# braiding the Balkans

# CHATHAM HOUSE PAPERS

A Soviet Foreign Policy Programme Publication
Programme Director: Neil Malcolm

The Royal Institute of International Affairs, at Chatham House in London, has provided an impartial forum for discussion and debate on current international issues for some 70 years. Its resident research fellows, specialized information resources, and range of publications, conferences, and meetings span the fields of international politics, economics, and security. The Institute is independent of government.

Chatham House Papers are short monographs on current policy problems which have been commissioned by the RIIA. In preparing the papers, authors are advised by a study group of experts convened by the RIIA, and publication of a paper indicates that the Institute regards it as an authoritative contribution to the public debate. The Institute does not, however, hold opinions of its own; the views expressed in this publication are the responsibility of the author.

CHATHAM HOUSE PAPERS

WITHDRAWN

# Remaking the Balkans

## Christopher Cviic

WITHDRAWN

The Royal Institute of International Affairs
Pinter Publishers
London

© Royal Institute of International Affairs, 1991

First published in Great Britain in 1991 by
Pinter Publishers Limited
25 Floral Street, London WC2E 9DS

**British Library Cataloguing in Publication Data**

A CIP catalogue record for this book is available from the British Library

ISBN 0-86187-086-7 (Paperback)
     0-86187-085-9 (Hardback)



Reproduced from copy supplied by
Koinonia Limited
Printed and bound in Great Britain by
Biddles Ltd

# CONTENTS

**Maps**

# PREFACE

The idea of writing a Chatham House Paper on the Balkans was suggested to me in the spring of 1990 by William Wallace, the then Deputy
Director and Director of Studies at the Royal Institute of International
Affairs. I doubted whether, at a time when momentous changes were
taking place in the better-known Central Europe and the Soviet Union,
there would be interest in a work on the Balkans. But he persuaded me
that there would be and I accepted his invitation to write such a study. In
the event it proved to be a prescient idea on his part.

After William Wallace's departure from the Institute at the end of
1990 to take up a post at St Antony's College, Oxford, the idea of a
Chatham House Paper on the Balkans continued to be supported and
encouraged by Jonathan Stern, the Acting Director of Studies. Others at
the Royal Institute of International Affairs to whom I owe particular
thanks for support and encouragement are Pauline Wickham, the Institute's Head of Publications, and Neil Malcolm, Head of its Soviet
Programme.

I am much indebted to all those other colleagues at the Institute and
friends outside who attended the two study groups and provided informa-
tion and helpful comment on the manuscript, in many cases in writing.
Here I must particularly mention Liliana Brisby, Richard Crampton,
Richard Davy, Kenneth Duke, Jonathan Eyal, Peter Ferdinand, George
Fodor, James Gow, Janet Gunn, Sir Reginald Hibbert, Roland Jovanovic,
Anne Lane, Karl Lavrencic, Michèle Ledic, Margie Lindsay, Malcolm
Mackintosh, David Madden, Branka Magas, Neil Malcolm, Charles
Meynell, James Pettifer, Philip Robins, Libor Roucek, George Schöpflin,

*Preface*

Gerald Segal, Geoffrey Stern, Trevor Taylor, Helen Wallace and David Wedgwood Benn. I must emphasize, however, that the opinions expressed here are my own, personal ones. Vladimir Pavlinic produced the maps, which should greatly assist in understanding the historical detail.

I am grateful to many other colleagues at the Institute, and particularly to staff in the two libraries. My special thanks are due to Shyama Iyer, the Soviet Programme Assistant, who was responsible for the organization of the study groups, the distribution of the manuscript and other important tasks; and to Margaret May of the Publications Department for her work on the editing and the production of the book. Lysèle Lathia, the Institute's Computer Manager, taught me how to use a word-processor and supported me generously during my long learning process. Last but by no means least, I acknowledge a very special debt of gratitude to Lieselotte Duvivier, my colleague on *The World Today*, who so willingly took many burdens off me during the rather hectic weeks when I was writing this study.

This work draws upon my postgraduate research in modern Yugoslav history many years ago at St Antony's College, Oxford, and the more recent experience, from 1969 to 1990, of reporting and analysing East and Central European affairs as a staff correspondent for *The Economist*.

*London, July 1991*                                        Christopher Cviic

# 1
# INTRODUCTION

With monotonous regularity, and some justification, writers on the Balkans have for years been echoing a famous film title: *Im Balkan nichts Neues* ('All Quiet in the Balkans'). The thesis of this study is that this has not been true for quite a while and that, since the end of the cold war and the dramatic retreat of Soviet power from Europe, momentous changes have been taking place in the Balkans, which have now come visibly to a head. Indeed, *Im Balkan viel Neues*: there is a lot of news from the Balkans.

What, then, is new in the region? Not, surely, the prospect of further fragmentation (or 'Balkanization') if, for example, Yugoslavia definitely breaks up? 'Balkanization' is, by definition, certainly nothing new in the Balkans. No, the really new – and, for all those interested in the area, exciting – thing is that, for the first time in their recent history, the people of the Balkans seem to be on their own, with no external powers trying to impose their will either on the region as a whole, or on any parts of it. The upheavals that are taking place there (and the attendant instability) are not being caused by external forces, as always happened in the past, but are occurring as a result of pressure from within, exerted by indigenous forces.

This study analyses some of those changes and suggests possible directions in which they may take the region. Four countries are dealt with here: Albania, Bulgaria, Romania and Yugoslavia. Apart from the fact that they are all situated in the Balkans, they have all, until recently, lived under communist rule since the end of World War II – unlike the other two Balkan countries, Greece and Turkey.

1

Neither of these countries is considered in depth in this study, largely because of their ambiguous status. Greece, halfway between the Balkans and Western Europe, is a member of Nato and the European Community on the one hand, but is also deeply involved in Balkan politics and in various intra-Balkan projects. Turkey, likewise, is a Nato member (though remaining so far only an aspirant to full Community membership); its history and geographical position, however, also give it an important stake both in the Balkans and in the Middle East.[1]

No analysis of the present situation makes sense without an idea of what has led up to it – particularly how the attempt of the post-1945 communist rulers at appropriating ('communizing') nationalism ended up with communism being nationalized, and how this still further aggravated the old problems the communists had inherited. This recent historical background is provided in Chapters 2 and 3. Chapter 4 deals with the dismal economic legacy of the communist era.

The fact that that legacy can now be tackled is due to the ending of the cold war in 1989–90, which has resulted in a strategic downgrading of the Balkans in East–West relations. With the release of the external corset that had gripped the whole of Eastern and Central Europe, including the Balkans, throughout the whole cold war era, many long-suppressed national aspirations have pushed themselves up to the top of the political agenda and have become of concern to the rest of Europe. This is particularly true of Yugoslavia. Chapter 5 looks at the reasons for the current crisis there and its possible outcome. Chapter 6 discusses the implications for the rest of Europe of the changes now taking place in the Balkans and describes some of the policy dilemmas these changes pose for individual governments as well as for the European Community, the Council of Europe and other institutions.

This Chatham House Paper should be read in conjunction with two others published earlier this year: *East Central Europe from Reform to Transformation*, by Judy Batt, which analyses the political and economic changes in Central Europe in 1989–90 and the process that preceded it; and *The European Community and Eastern Europe*, by John Pinder, which charts the evolution of the European Community's policy towards Central and Eastern Europe and examines some of the policy opportunities and dilemmas facing it in the area now.

If this study appears to be too 'Yugocentric', then that is partly because it is written by a Croat from Yugoslavia (living in Britain since 1954), but also, and even more, because Yugoslavia is the epicentre of the series of political earthquakes that are shaking this whole quake-prone area. Fortunately, it is highly unlikely that another world war will be sparked off by any of the current Balkan disputes, however bloody and nasty. But, as the following pages attempt to demonstrate, one thing is certain: the Balkans will continue to matter in a variety of ways to Europe and the rest of the world, and therefore deserve close outside attention.

# 2

# COMMUNISTS AS NATIONALISTS

On the face of it, the introduction of communist rule in the Balkans after 1945 represented a fundamental break with the past. The area's new rulers, in line with the ideas of Marx, Engels and Lenin, proclaimed their allegiance to the principle of 'proletarian internationalism' as the antithesis of the nationalism that had pervaded Eastern Europe under the prewar regimes. What actually happened was that even in the new power context, within the limits imposed by Soviet control, these supposedly internationalist-minded leaders continued to pursue the traditional national objectives of their individual countries.

The difference was that the pre-communist rulers were free to express their patriotism and, indeed, found it advantageous to flaunt it – it made them more popular with their own people. Their communist successors did not have this freedom: if they wanted to play the national card, they had to do so discreetly, in code, as prescribed by communist protocol.

One of the most important rules was that, whatever happened in practice, appearances had to be preserved. There was a good reason for this. To manipulate nationalism in a pragmatic way was one thing – and was broadly acceptable. To espouse nationalism openly was not, because it involved the risk of undermining the Marxist–Leninist ideology, the basis of all the communist regimes' claim to legitimacy. None of the communist leaders dared take that risk. Thus, though the practice had in effect become pure *Realpolitik*, not significantly different from that in the pre-communist era, it continued to be pursued in a communist guise.

For example, the idea that class was the basic category of domestic as well as international politics (expressed in the principle of 'proletarian

internationalism') continued to be upheld. Within multinational Yugoslavia, the safely Marxist equivalent to 'proletarian internationalism' was
the principle of *bratstvo i jedinstvo* (brotherhood and unity). This satis-
fied the unwritten rule, observed by members of the Soviet bloc and non-
aligned Yugoslav communists alike, that where ideological compro-
mises had to be made, the necessary 're-positioning' had to be kept
within the broad Marxist confines. Later on, as individual communist
leaders felt more and more compelled to broaden the base of their
support, nationalism became effectively 're-legitimized' in one communist-ruled country after another. Internationalist 'class' rhetoric was
increasingly discarded in favour of an open appeal to national sentiment.

All this was ironic, perhaps, but hardly surprising. In the Balkans, as
in the whole of Eastern and Central Europe, communism never stood a
chance of bypassing, let alone supplanting, nationalism. It is not difficult
to see why. Nation rather than class has been the main political category
throughout the region's recent history and still is today. This is no
temporary aberration but the result of centuries of experience.

## Old nations, new states
The peoples of Eastern and Central Europe, including of course those of
the Balkans, are old nations, many of which had once lived in states of
their own. But this (often lovingly embellished) 'golden' era of independent statehood was followed by subjection to foreign rule, in some
cases lasting many centuries. The four dynastic empires which between
them ruled Eastern and Central Europe – the Austrian, the Prussian, the
Ottoman and the Russian – were all hostile to the idea of the national
state, so independent statehood had to be fought for and was gained (or
regained, as those concerned would see it) by most of those nations only
recently – by some as late as the end of World War I. The political map
of Eastern and Central Europe still reflects the order imposed in the
aftermath of that war by the victorious Entente powers: Britain, France,
Italy and the United States. That order was enshrined in a series of peace
treaties – the best known of which, signed in June 1919 at Versailles,
gave its name to the whole of the post-1918 settlement in Europe.

These peace treaties left much 'unfinished business' behind. The
principle of national self-determination, affirmed by President Woodrow
Wilson in his famous Fourteen Points of January 1918 and adopted as
one of the Entente's war aims, was not fully implemented. Millions were
left separated from their 'home nation'. Not all the nations of Eastern and

Map 1 The Balkans in 1815

© Vladimir Pavlinic, 1991

Central Europe which aspired to independent statehood achieved it at that time. But the aspiration lived on and is still there, in some cases felt even more passionately and supported more broadly today than in the post-1918 period. Why is there still this striving for – indeed, to many Western eyes, obsession with – independent statehood? And now, of all times, when Western Europe, for example, is moving in the opposite direction, towards greater integration?

The answer lies in the Eastern and Central European peoples' unique historical experience. In Western Europe, most of the major nations have for generations now felt secure in their identity within their established nation-states. By contrast, insecurity has been the rule in Eastern and Central Europe, and particularly in the Balkans. All the nations of that region have at some time in the past (and especially the recent past) seen their national identity, language and historical culture threatened. The old empires were by no means perfect, but the national states that followed them were almost invariably worse.

The Habsburg empire, in fact, operated on the principle of upholding the historic rights of established states. These rights included broad religious and national toleration. The introduction of the Patent of Toleration by Emperor Joseph II in 1781 enshrined an already existing practice. Under the Ottoman empire, there existed in the Balkans the so-called *millet* system of semi-autonomous religious–national communities. The Muslim *millet* embraced no unified territory nor any homogeneous ethnic group or people of the same political and legal status. It held a position of superiority over the others because it was the only one which shared the religion and the laws of the ruling Ottoman class and its material aid. The non-Muslims were on their own, so to speak: they were free to organize their religious, legal and educational institutions, but only from their own resources. In that sense the system held the non-Muslims back, but at the same time it enabled them to preserve their ethnic and religious identity under the leadership of the church. In the Ottoman empire this meant the Orthodox church, which the rulers found a comfortable partner and, very important, a useful Christian counterweight to the Roman Catholic church, that strong and active supporter of Europe's resistance to Ottoman invasions. That was how religion and identity became inextricably linked, and how the Orthodox church assumed its extremely important role in the public life of the individual Balkan nations.

The real threat to national identities came in the last decades of these two empires: in the Habsburg empire the Slavs felt threatened by the

7

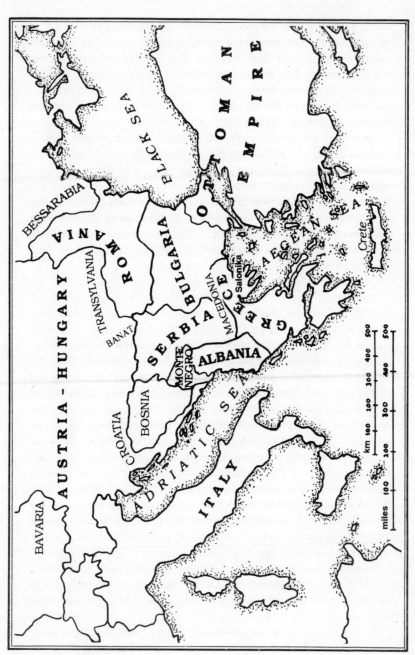

© Vladimir Pavlinic, 1991

Map 2 The Balkans in 1914

newly awakened German and Hungarian nationalism, and in the Ottoman empire the non-Turks saw as the main threat the Young Turks, who were looking for ways of creating a modern Ottoman identity. Moreover, in the more confined space of some of the new nation-states established after both empires broke up, minorities became exposed to a variety of dangers – from discrimination and assimilation to expulsion or even physical annihilation. Indeed, for some nations, such as the Albanians or the Macedonians, predatory neighbours not all that much bigger or more numerous than themselves have proved more deadly than the old empires ever were. The threat to the national identity of such peoples still exists today. Not surprisingly, this has helped to strengthen the bonds linking members of each individual nation to one another at the expense of class and ideological or even religious bonds. This has always posed special problems for adherents of universalist ideologies – such as communism, for example.

## Marx's error

In their Communist Manifesto, Marx and Engels wrote, 'The workers have no country.' Being political realists, they accepted that the proletarian revolution would occur within a national framework, within individual states. But they did not see nations continuing after the revolution. 'National differences and antagonisms between peoples are vanishing gradually from day to day,' the Manifesto declared, and 'the supremacy of the proletariat will cause them to vanish still faster.'[2] Marx and Engels relegated the question of nationality to merely peripheral status even though it remained an important issue, for example, in Germany and Italy, which had still not achieved unification. Marx and Engels placed their hopes in the internationalist class-consciousness of Western Europe's industrial proletariat. Their calculations were put to the test in World War I and proved wrong: the socialist parties in Europe voted almost unanimously for the credits needed by their 'bourgeois' governments to prosecute what any Marxist worth his salt would have designated – as Lenin did – as an imperialist war.

In Central and Eastern Europe, by contrast, the socialists, however hard they tried, were never able to sidestep, let alone ignore, the 'national factor'. There was a good reason for this. As the ideology of socialism began to spread, national feeling grew in strength among the diverse peoples of the Russian and Habsburg empires and in the new states arising out of the crumbling Ottoman empire. The socialists of the

Habsburg empire, whether they liked it or not, were obliged to take into account the national aspirations of the peoples they were working amongst. In the relatively democratic conditions that prevailed there, socialists had to compete for votes like everybody else. Universal franchise and the secret ballot had been achieved in the Austrian half of the empire by 1907, and cautious democratization was beginning to take off in the Hungarian half as well. The situation forced the socialists to allow for national party organizations. Thus, by the beginning of the twentieth century there were in the ramshackle Habsburg empire separate social democratic parties for the Czechs, Italians, Poles, Romanians, Slovenes and Romanians as well as the German-speaking population. Not at all surprisingly, socialist leaders in Austria–Hungary, like Otto Bauer and Karl Renner, devoted much energy and attention to devising ways of resolving the multinational empire's ethnic conflicts.

The national question also posed problems for socialists in the Russian empire. But the conditions here were far more repressive. As a small, conspiratorial party made up of professional revolutionaries, Lenin's Bolsheviks did not have to make concessions to national sentiment. There were no votes that needed to be chased. The Bolsheviks could – and did – appeal to national sentiment in their propaganda in Russia before World War I but only as a tactical expedient, without ever 'legitimizing' it. Lenin saw that nationalism could be used, in certain circumstances, to aid the cause of the revolution. But Bolshevik support for national causes had to be 'strictly limited to what is progressive in such movements'.[3]

It was entirely in this light that Lenin saw the right of a nation to 'self-determination'. There were certain conditions under which separation of a nation from the state was 'progressive' and others under which it was not. The crucial point was that it was the party which decided what was and was not progressive. Lenin shrugged off the objections of those like Rosa Luxemburg who argued that the principle of self-determination for non-Russian nationalities would, for example, deliver Poland to the control of the landlords and the bourgeoisie, and bring the Muslim population in Central Asia under the thumb of the feudal chiefs and religious leaders. What mattered to Lenin was the immediate need: the party should be able to mobilize the powerful appeal of nationalism against the tsarist state. Later on, in power, the victorious proletariat (or, rather, the party on its behalf) would judge demands for self-determination in the light of the broader, 'class' interest. And so it proved.

The federal system created under Lenin and perfected under Stalin was merely a façade covering a monolithic, centralized state. The Soviet system paid lip-service to equality for all the nations and provided for the preservation of national cultures and languages, but only to the extent that these supported Soviet, not national, policy aims. Even where local nationals held political office in the republics and other territories of the federation, Moscow always exercised absolute control – usually through the device of having a Russian as a second-in-command. It continued to pursue a long-term, though never openly declared, policy of Russification, sometimes openly stressing and at other times playing down the theory of the ultimate amalgamation of nations.

### Comintern and the Balkans

In the period before World War II, communist parties in the Balkans were operating under several handicaps. One was that, being 'subversive' and revolutionary, they were subject to intense police pressure and forced to work in conditions of illegality. This made them even more dependent on, and constrained by, the line laid down by the Communist International (Comintern) in Moscow. The Comintern's policy was guided by the strategic and tactical interests of the Soviet state. Local political considerations were taken into account but played only a secondary role. In some cases, the Comintern's line made the local communist parties' task of winning support among their fellow-nationals easier, in others more difficult.

For example, Romania's Communist Party had a particularly hard time of it. Its main political handicap was that, because of its dependence on the Soviet Union, a country seen by most Romanians as a hostile neighbour, it was regarded by the population at large as 'anti-national'. This was perhaps inevitable in a country which had done well out of World War I and was worried that its neighbours might seek to deprive it of its territorial gains (Transylvania, a part of Banat and northern Bukruja from Austria–Hungary; southern Dobruja from Bulgaria; and Bessarabia from Russia). The party was further damaged in the eyes of the Romanian population because (for important historical reasons) it largely comprised Jews, Hungarians and members of other minorities, rather than ethnic Romanians.

For a party already branded as an agent of a foreign power, the annexation of Bessarabia by the Soviet Union in 1940 and its amalgamation with what was then known as the Moldavian Soviet Republic was nothing short of a disaster. Comintern discipline prevented the Romanian

Party from opposing the annexation, thus putting it even more at odds with the rest of the nation. It is not surprising in the circumstances that a strongly nationalist and recently humiliated country actually welcomed the Romanian government's decision to join the war against the Soviet Union on Hitler's side in 1941.

The war enabled Romania not only to regain Bessarabia but also to annex extra territories (including Odessa) in the east, which had never been Romanian. The area was called Transnistria and placed under a Romanian governor. This was Hitler's compensation to Romania for its loss of northern Transylvania, which had been 'awarded' to Hungary in August 1940 by Germany and Italy. In August 1944, when King Michael's coup brought Romania over to the Allies' side, the Romanian Communist Party had fewer than a thousand members. It could hardly have been otherwise: the party had nothing significant to contribute to what most Romanians, rightly or wrongly, considered as the most important item on the national agenda.

## The Balkan Federation plan

Another example of the impact on the Balkan communists of the Comintern's policies was its advocacy in the 1920s and early 1930s of a Balkan Federation to replace Yugoslavia and other surrounding national states. Yugoslavia was a pillar of the French-backed cordon sanitaire in Eastern Europe, which was anti-German but also anti-communist. Yugoslavia's King Alexander, a former page at the Russian imperial court at St Petersburg, provided refuge and generous material support in Yugoslavia for thousands of post-1917 anti-communist Russian exiles. This help even included setting up and maintaining an officers' school for cadets who had escaped to Yugoslavia after 1917. Even after the king's assassination in 1934, Yugoslavia continued its anti-communist policy and was one of the last European states to establish diplomatic relations with the Soviet Union – in 1940.

## Reaction to the plan

The Comintern's plan for a break-up of Yugoslavia and its replacement by a Balkan Federation was popular in *Bulgaria*. The reasons were obvious: there was widespread resentment over the loss to Yugoslavia after 1918 of the bulk of Macedonia, regarded by Bulgarians as their land, and over the consequent influx of large numbers of refugees from the so-called Vardar Macedonia, including Skopje, that had come under the new Yugoslav state. In addition other refugees arrived from Thrace, which Greece had taken after World War I. In the early 1930s, 11 per cent of Sofia's population consisted of post-1918 refugees from those two areas (not including children born to these refugees after their arrival in Bulgaria).

To Bulgarian eyes, the possibility of reopening the Macedonian issue via the idea of a Balkan Federation was attractive. For the Bulgarian Communist Party, which was much stronger and better organized than its Romanian counterpart, the idea represented good tactics. Unlike in Romania, there was a strong pro-Russian sentiment, particularly among the peasants and the less educated, dating back to Bulgaria's liberation by Russia from Ottoman role in the 1877–8 Russo–Turkish war.

For the communists in *Greece* next door, Macedonia was a big headache. The party's advocacy, in line with Comintern's policy, of an autonomous Macedonian state within a Balkan Federation undermined all its efforts to broaden its political influence among the Greek people. Such a state would include the Greek portion of Macedonia, inhabited by almost 1.5m Greeks, of whom some 700,000 were refugees from Asia Minor, resettled after the 1921–2 Greek–Turkish war. The Greek communists' difficulties were compounded by the prospect that a future Balkan Federation would also involve autonomy for Greece's Western Thrace province: some of the Muslim population here regard themselves as Turks. The issue of Macedonia has continued to dog the Greek Left up to the present day.

In *Yugoslavia* itself, the picture was more complicated. The idea of the Yugoslav state's break-up into separate national units and their inclusion in a broader Balkan Federation held an obvious appeal for many of the country's non-Serbs, who saw the Yugoslav kingdom* – with its Serbian king (Alexander) and Serbian-dominated army and civil service – as Greater Serbia by another name.

It was precisely in Yugoslav *Macedonia* that the Balkan Federation project gained the communists strong political support. Officially designated as 'Southern Serbia' after 1918, Macedonia was exposed to systematic Serbianization. One of the features of this policy was the state-sponsored and heavily subsidized colonization by ethnic Serbs (including ex-soldiers) from other parts of Yugoslavia. The communists' popularity in Macedonia was reflected in the 1920 election for the Yugoslav Constituent Assembly: they got 38 per cent of the vote and

---

*The unitary kingdom of Serbs, Croats and Slovenes, which came into being in December 1918, formally adopted the name Yugoslavia ('Yugo' meaning 'South') in October 1929.

emerged as the strongest party. (Later on, the communists lost much of this support, chiefly because of factional struggles in their own ranks among pro-Bulgarian, pro-Serb and outright Macedonian factions.)

In *Croatia*, too, where opposition to Serbian hegemony in the new state was strong, the communists achieved good electoral results before the party was banned in 1921. Later the Communist Party lost most of its original gains to the Croatian Peasant Party, which became the main channel for both national and social discontent among the Croats under its charismatic leader, Stjepan Radic.*

In *Slovenia*, the political scene was dominated by two 'bourgeois' parties, one liberal and one Catholic, and there was little antagonism to Belgrade before 1941. The Communist Party was widely regarded as a fringe organization far removed from mainstream political activity. But the communists began to be taken more seriously when, in 1937, they set up a separate Slovene Communist Party within the Yugoslav Party (a parallel move was made in Croatia) and began to take up Slovene national concerns, such as the fear of German and Italian expansionism, within a broader anti-fascist framework. Neither the Slovene nor the Croat Party had any organizational independence, but the very fact of their existence made recruitment easier.

Within *Serbia*, communism benefited from the strong pro-Russian feelings that prevailed. As in Bulgaria, this was based on gratitude for backing in the past, not least in 1914, by the great Slav Orthodox power. It was reinforced by the Serbian habit of studying in Russia, and was relatively easily converted after 1917 into support for Soviet Russia among the younger generation.

But even those Serbs who – like the communists – were opposed to the monarchist regime never warmed to the idea of the break-up of the state and relished even less that of teaming up in a Balkan Federation with Serbia's next-door neighbour and bitter rival, Bulgaria. The Comintern line on Yugoslavia presented difficulties for those like Sima Markovic, Party Secretary in the 1920s, who – though personally indifferent to the nationality issue – were aware of its unpopularity among the Serbs. Markovic tried to cope with it by 'relativizing' nationality conflicts in Yugoslavia, portraying them as essentially a masked struggle over the distribution of

*Radic died in August 1928, two months after being shot in the National Assembly in Belgrade by a Montenegrin deputy, Punisa Racic, who also murdered two other Croat deputies and wounded two others. In spite of this multiple murder, Racic got off lightly, with a sentence which he served in an open prison. It was only after 1945 that the communists sentenced him to death for collaboration with the Nazis during World War II and executed him.

14

wealth between the 'national bourgeoisies': the Serb one eager to overcome its own backwardness and wrest the dominant position in the
country's economic and financial system from the more advanced capitalist Croat and Slovene bourgeoisies. These, in turn, according to this
reading of the Yugoslav situation, were trying to force Serbia to stay a
purely agrarian country. This intriguing and ingenious attempt to
'explain away' the nationality conflict in Yugoslavia failed to convince,
not least because, for example, the bulk of the capital in Croatia and
Slovenia was foreign.* In the mid-1930s, when the Comintern changed
its line to support for an anti-fascist coalition of states, it longer
advocated the break-up of Yugoslavia. There was a broad welcome for
the new line among the Serb Party members and sympathizers.

A similar situation obtained in *Montenegro*, one of the Communist
Party's strongest constituencies in Yugoslavia. There, as in Serbia, pro-
Russian sentiment dated back to pre-1918 days when Montenegro, a tiny
Christian Orthodox principality, received much political and material
backing from Russia. This sentiment was later transferred to Soviet
Russia.

### The Kosovo conundrum

There were only a handful of Communist Party members before World
War II among Yugoslavia's ethnic Albanians who, with the Macedonians, were the country's worst-treated national group. Concentrated in
Kosovo and Western Macedonia, the Albanians were subjected by the
Serbian authorities to systematic discrimination and various forms of
pressure, including pressure to leave *en masse*. In 1940, a year after the
signing of the Molotov–Ribbentrop Pact and the abandonment of the
Popular Front line, the Yugoslav Party took a first step towards making
it possible to recruit Kosovo Albanians: organizational autonomy was
granted to the party committee for Kosovo, which had previously been
under the regional party committee for Montenegro.

When in April 1941 Yugoslavia was invaded and dismembered by
Germany and Italy, assisted by Bulgaria and Hungary, nowhere was the
end of the Yugoslav state welcomed more warmly than among the
Kosovo Albanians. And when, after the German attack on the Soviet

---

*An updated version of this theory was widely used by Serbian communist writers, with
the same political aim of 'relativizing' the nationality question in Yugoslavia, in the
1970s and 1980s. They represented the current nationality conflicts in Yugoslavia as
nothing more than 'turf fights' among the 'national politocracies' in individual republics.

Union in June 1941, Yugoslav communists began to organize guerrilla resistance, many local Serbs were ready to respond – but no ethnic Albanians. Participation in any struggle involving a return to Yugoslav (which, to the Albanians, meant Serbian) rule was anathema to the Albanians. 'Even the name "Yugoslavia" repels potential Party supporters', reported Svetozar Vukmanovic-Tempo, a senior Yugoslav Party official sent to the area to see what could be done.[4]

In Albania itself, there was no Communist Party proper before World War II, only some half a dozen groups of various ideological shades in the main towns. The most important of these turned out to be the one to which Enver Hoxha, the country's future ruler, belonged, in Korca in the south. The Communist Party of Albania (CPA), later renamed the Albanian Party of Labour, was formed, with help from the Communist Party of Yugoslavia (CPY), only in November 1941, after the Soviet Union had been invaded by Germany and the anti-fascist war provided a platform on which to unite. Enver Hoxha became its leader. The motivation of the CPY seems to have been that recruitment in Kosovo could perhaps be facilitated if it established a subordinate, auxiliary Albanian Party.

Kosovo, portions of western Macedonia and an area on the eastern border of Montenegro had, meanwhile, been incorporated by the Axis powers into the new Greater Albania under Italian tutelage. The Italians provided food and arms and a measure of local autonomy. This removed from the Albanians any strong national motive for resistance. Nevertheless, resistance to the Italians did begin under the leadership of one or two chieftains. In 1942, Enver Hoxha and the fledgling CPA managed to join up with those chieftains to create the Movement of National Liberation (LNC). The communists seized the leadership of it from the start. Most of the country's chieftains and leaders stayed aloof, however. When they saw the leftist tendency of the LNC, they set up a rival and potentially stronger grouping called the Balli Kombetar (BK).

The Yugoslav Party criticized the CPA for having formed the LNC on too narrow a basis. In the summer of 1943, when it looked as if Italy was going to be knocked out of the war and Albania would be liberated, the Albanian communists responded to this criticism by trying to negotiate a common front between the LNC and the BK. An agreement was reached at Mukje in August 1943. It included a demand for self-determination in Kosovo – a *sine qua non* for every Albanian nationalist. However, this was unacceptable to the Albanian Party's Yugoslav mentors, and Hoxha was forced to side with them and overturn the agreement, anathematizing the BK.

The rapid intervention of the Germans after the capitulation of Italy prevented the LNC from obtaining all the arms and equipment it needed for its newly forming partisan battalions. During the winter of 1943–4 successive German drives, actively or passively supported by the BK, wiped out the partisan units in the centre and north of Albania and nearly destroyed the new battalions in the south. But as spring approached, the destruction spread by the Germans and the BK stimulated recruitment for the partisans. They rapidly eclipsed the BK, gaining enough strength to muster a small army to strike back in the centre and the north.

One of the few chieftains who were founder-members of the LNC was Abas Kupi. After the Mukje fiasco, he broke away from the LNC and founded his own Zogist movement.* With the failure of the BK, he became the great hope for a 'nationalist' resistance in Albania; but the resistance never materialized. The British, insisting on resistance before supply, helped the LNC/partisans. Kupi, demanding supply, recognition of King Zog and the promise of self-determination for Kosovo before resistance, had failed to meet British requirements before the partisans, in their northwards drive, overran his territory. The Albanian National Resistance Army (ANLA), led by Enver Hoxha, swept the board and set up a government which was completely in the hands of the CPA.

At this point, in the autumn of 1944, the intention of the CPY that the CPA should be a subordinate party began to cause friction. A new envoy from Tito intervened in the proceedings of the CPA's Politburo from October onwards and played an assertive part in the plenum of the novice CPA's Central Committee in November. He was critical of the CPA's (i.e., Hoxha's) line during the war. Hoxha, with the ANLA behind him, was too powerful in the moment of victory to be overthrown; but the Yugoslavs had the support of the second strong man in the CPA, Koci Xoxe, who had sided with them unhesitatingly at the time of the Mukje affair. The struggle for control of the party and hence of Albania continued until 1948. It was about to end in triumph for Xoxe and the Yugoslavs when Stalin's break with Tito unexpectedly handed victory to Hoxha.

Meanwhile, at the end of the war, Kosovo had become a contentious issue between the CPA and CPY. Already, towards the end of 1943, Vukmanovic-Tempo had accused Enver Hoxha and his close colleague, Haxhi Lleshi, of overt Albanian chauvinism, which may explain why Hoxha was so quick to adopt the Yugoslav line at Mukje. In the autumn

*Supporters of King Zog, who went into exile after Mussolini's invasion of Albania in 1939.

of 1944, the Yugoslavs had problems in 'liberating' Kosovo. The Albanians were brought in to make the task easier – in other words, Albanians would be 'liberated' by other Albanians. The ANLA sent two brigades into Kosovo in October 1944 and the force was raised to two divisions by the end of the year. The Yugoslavs contrived to move the Albanian forces out by the spring of 1945, and full Yugoslav control was then imposed on 'liberated' Kosovo, dashing any hopes on the part of the Kosovars of self-determination in favour of Albania. Enver Hoxha and his close supporters in Albania had to swallow the fact that they had been 'used' in this way by the CPY. It seems to have made them determined that, if Yugoslavia had Kosovo, it would not – if they could help it – have Albania as well.[3]

## Yugoslavia's wartime agendas

In Yugoslavia, too, World War II was only partially the epic anti-fascist struggle that conventional history portrays. A closer look reveals a number of (often carefully concealed) national agendas. It could be argued that Tito owed his victory in 1944–5 above all to his understanding of these national concerns and to his skilful exploitation of them for his own non-nationalist power-seeking ends.

Tito certainly made mistakes but he also learnt from them. An example was his proclamation of a Soviet-style republic in western Serbia in the autumn of 1941. This failed to ignite the broader, all-Yugoslav revolution he was hoping for and made it easy for the Germans to eject the communists from there. National concerns predominated in Serbia at the time, ensuring that it remained out of the communists' reach until 1944, when the Red Army reached it from the east and liberated Belgrade, with the Yugoslav partisans' assistance. During the intervening period, Serbia stayed under the overall control of the Germans and the Vichy-style Serbian government of General Milan Nedic that they had installed.

The third player in this complex relationship was General Draza Mihailovic, who started the first resistance to the Germans in May 1941 with a guerrilla force, popularly known as Cetniks, and was appointed Minister of War by the royalist Yugoslav government in exile in London. He negotiated with Tito about the possibility of uniting their efforts, but owing to the two leaders' completely different long-term aims (and hence proposed tactics), the attempt failed and they became the bitterest of enemies. After Tito's forces were expelled from Serbia by the

Germans, Mihailovic ended up by operating what amounted to an informal understanding with the Nedic regime – justified by the need to preserve Serbia from the destruction likely to be inflicted on it by German reprisals for serious guerrilla resistance.

Mihailovic's strategy was based on the calculation that, as in World War I, Serbia would be liberated by the victorious Western allies marching from the direction of Salonika or, perhaps, the Adriatic coast. This suited the Germans who, though opposed to Mihailovic, realized that the joint efforts of Nedic and Mihailovic successfully kept the communists out of Serbia. They were able to do so because the majority of the *Srbijanci*, Serbs from Serbia proper (*uza Srbija*),* decided that a policy of lying low was better suited to Serbia's national interests. At any rate, they felt it to be preferable to the communists' apparently reckless revolutionism, which many feared would lead to savage reprisals by the occupying forces and wholesale destruction of property.

Behind this lay the perception of many Serbs (and certainly of the Cetniks) that their most dangerous enemies in Yugoslavia were not actually the Germans, the Italians and their allies, the Bulgarians and the Hungarians, but rather the other Yugoslavs, particularly the Croats (whether wearing partisan uniforms or those of the puppet regime), the Bosnian Muslims and the Albanians. The so-called Ustasa ('insurgent') regime of Ante Pavelic first of all tried to expel the bulk of the Croat Serbs to German-occupied Serbia. When the Germans stopped further transports to Serbia because this was causing them political problems there, the Ustasas sent to concentration camps huge numbers of Serbs (together with Jews, gypsies and anti-Pavelic Croats). Many thousands of Serbs (the exact figures are disputed) were killed in the wartime fascist Croat state; many others were expelled to Serbia proper.[6] This experience had a traumatic effect on Serbian consciousness and continued to form political perceptions afterwards. It is possible that a free and open debate among the peoples of Yugoslavia in the immediate aftermath of World War II about what actually happened between 1941 and 1945 – particularly about who did what to whom (including murders of Croats and Muslims by Serbian Cetniks) could have dispelled some of the myths and moderated some of the hatreds generated by that period. However, the imposition of a heavily doctored communist version of events allowed the wartime hatreds to fester, feeding on the new grievances of the Tito era.

*They are often differentiated from Serbs from 'over there' (*preko*) in Croatia and Bosnia, who are called *Precani*.

The Mihailovic movement's decision to adopt an essentially wait-and-see policy, combining collaboration with low-level resistance to the occupying forces by locally recruited Cetniks, had serious long-term consequences. Collaboration with the Italians and sometimes even the Germans – and, after 1942, the participation of Cetnik units in German and Italian operations against the Tito partisans – discredited the movement in the eyes of the British, whose main interest was short-term: the actual military struggle on the ground against the Axis powers. To this end they were ready to support whoever was prepared to kill the most Germans. This, of course, ruled out from the start those anti-communists in Slovenia, Croatia and Serbia itself who (whether out of conviction or purely tactically) had openly aligned themselves with the Axis powers. But it also sank the Cetniks, although the British reached the decision to stop backing them with the utmost reluctance and relatively late – towards the end of 1943. The loss of British support was a body blow to the Cetniks, politically as much as militarily. By the same token, British military and political backing was one of the key elements of the partisans' ultimate victory.

There were in fact three reasons why the British dropped Mihailovic in favour of Tito. In the first place, Tito had convinced them that, unlike Mihailovic, he was a serious military ally against the Germans. But he had also given a strong impression that, also unlike Mihailovic and his largely Serb Cetniks, he and his partisan movement enjoyed broad support among all the Yugoslav nations. Finally, his forces controlled a much larger liberated territory.

As regards the first reason, there is a 'revisionist' school of thought which argues that the decision to switch from Mihailovic to Tito was a tragic mistake, due partly to over-optimistic reports by certain British liaison officers on Tito's military capabilities, partly to deliberate pro-Tito and anti-Mihailovic disinformation by communists and fellow-travellers in key British organizations such as the Special Operations Executive (SOE).[7]

The present vigorous debate about who was or was not really fighting the Germans and why, and about the communists' actual role in the British change of policy is still in full spate. More evidence is needed before any conclusive judgments can be reached. As far as Tito's military contribution is concerned, it does look as if it may have been overestimated. The Germans never kept large formations in Yugoslavia (if one excludes those withdrawing from Greece and Albania in 1944 and early 1945). As for the Italians, it is true that in the summer of 1943 they had more than 300,000 troops stationed – or tied down, as some would have it – in Yugoslavia. But those Italian troops were there not primarily for military reasons – to fight the insurgents – but above all to provide visible back-up for Italy's position, conceded by Hitler, as a hegemonic power in the Western Balkans.

As to the second question – which movement was more broadly based – it is incontrovertible that Mihailovic was politically hamstrung by his pan-Serb programme, which envisaged the purging of 'Serb lands' (including Bosnia and Hercegovina and large parts of Croatia) of non-Serbs. In contrast, Tito led a broad coalition made up of Serbs and non-Serbs alike. In addition to ideological anti-fascists from among all nationalities, this attracted:

(a) *Slovenes*, whose country was split between the Third Reich and Mussolini's Italy and whose survival, as a nation, was threatened in Hitler's 'new order'.

(b) *Serbs* from Croatia and Bosnia and Hercegovina, threatened with annihilation by the Ustasa regime. But not all of the Croat Serbs, fleeing from Pavelic's terror, ended up in Tito's partisan ranks. Some of them joined the Cetniks, especially in the Italian-occupied areas in the south, notably around Knin. The Italian authorities financed and armed them as auxiliary forces to keep the partisans out but also to prevent the then Croat government from asserting its authority in Croat areas under Italian military occupation but not formally annexed by Italy.

(c) *Croats*, first from areas in the south annexed by Italy and then, from 1942 onwards, also elsewhere. The partisans' most important reservoir of recruitment consisted of Croats called up to serve in the regular Croat army – the so-called Domobrans (or 'defenders of the homeland') – who regularly handed themselves over to Tito in large numbers, together with their officers, weapons and equipment. The partisans were greatly helped by the Croats' reaction against Cetnik atrocities, particularly in southern Croatia and in Bosnia.

(d) *Bosnian Muslims*, wooed in vain by Pavelic, who called them 'the flower of the Croat nation' and even built a mosque for them in Zagreb, Croatia's predominantly Catholic capital. Very soon, even the Muslims originally attracted by Pavelic started to cool off, disillusioned by the brutal nature of his regime. What attracted many of them to Tito was the promise of autonomy for Bosnia and Hercegovina and, as in the case of the Croats, the need for protection against the strongly anti-Muslim Cetniks.

21

(e) *Macedonians*, disillusioned with Bulgarian rule and attracted by Tito's promise of a Macedonian republic within a postwar Yugoslav federation.

(f) *Kosovo Albanians*, who had been talked with difficulty, very late on, into joining Tito by communists from Albania holding out the prospect of joining Albania proper.

Tito's nationality policy, though more successful than that of his domestic rivals, nevertheless came under strain within the party itself at certain times. There was, for example, considerable tension in the wake of Yugoslavia's dismemberment in 1941 between the central Yugoslav Party leadership, which was committed to the continuance of the Yugoslav state in some form, and the party organization in Macedonia under Metodi Satorov, whose conspiratorial party name was 'Sarlo'. Satorov accepted the new territorial arrangement under which the bulk of Macedonia was incorporated into Bulgaria, broke organizational links with the Yugoslav Party and incorporated his regional committee into the Bulgarian Communist Party. At first, Tito sought to discipline Satorov, but without success. The dispute was ostensibly about jurisdiction but actually it was both about future frontiers between Balkan states and about the best tactics to pursue in organizing an insurrection (Satorov had argued that he could not raise support in Macedonia within a Yugoslav framework, which would recall to his fellow-Macedonians the pre-1941 Serbianization policy).

The issue eventually went to the Comintern for adjudication. In line with Stalin's cautious policy of not wishing to challenge the validity of Allied countries' borders, the Comintern decided in favour of the Yugoslav Party, which expelled Satorov. However, when he went to Bulgaria, the Communist Party there welcomed him into its leadership.

Later on in the war, the partisan movement in Croatia achieved considerable success under the leadership of Andrija Hebrang, a senior party figure and an able and intelligent organizer. In 1943–4 it controlled a large and well-run 'liberated territory' in Croatia. But the movement came under suspicion of having become 'too Croat'. The specific charge investigated by, among others, Milovan Djilas was that it was too ready to cooperate with the non-communist Croat opposition to Pavelic and generally to make concessions to Croat national feeling.

Tito was particularly infuriated when the Croat partisan movement set up its own, Croat, news agency on its large 'liberated' territory. He was also incensed by the Croat partisans' decision in September 1943 to announce, quite independently and without reference to the central Yugoslav leadership, the reunification with Croatia of territories ceded to Italy by royalist Yugoslavia under the 1920 Treaty of Rapallo, and of others ceded by Pavelic's regime under the so-called Venice Treaty of May 1941.

Hebrang argued that no other tactics were possible: one of the main criteria for success was sensitivity to the strong local national feeling. To no avail: after a high-level party investigation Hebrang was replaced by Vladimir Bakaric, a more junior and pliable man, dispatched to the just-liberated Belgrade in October 1944 and given a series of economic posts, without a strong power base. Hebrang was arrested in 1948, accused of siding with Stalin, and subsequently died in mysterious circumstances in prison, allegedly by committing suicide.*

### Paths to power

Not surprisingly, it took a good deal of Soviet effort to establish communist rule in Romania, where communism had been a marginal political force. The process was easier in Bulgaria, where there had been some wartime communist guerrilla resistance, but in both countries communist rule had clearly been imposed from outside. It was easier in Albania and Yugoslavia, where the local communists had managed to mobilize considerable support. The difference, crucial in an area such as the Balkans, was between those who had come to power by working with the grain of national feeling, as Tito had done in Yugoslavia and Hoxha in Albania, and those like the Bulgarian and Romanian communists, who owed their power totally to an external agency, Moscow.

### *Romania*

Of the four regimes, the Romanian was the weakest and therefore the most dependent on Moscow's backing. However, there were two factors that helped Romanian communists to consolidate their power. First,

---

*Later, the Yugoslav authorities produced documents purporting to show that Hebrang, who had been captured by the Pavelic police early in the war and subsequently exchanged for some high-ranking officials held by the partisans, had become a Pavelic spy 'turned' while in prison. New evidence brought to Zagreb from Belgrade in 1985 appears to confirm what had long been suspected: that the spying charge was a clumsy fabrication designed to blacken Hebrang's reputation posthumously. It also appears to confirm the widespread suspicion that he was murdered in prison. The non-communist Croat government elected in May 1990 has ordered a judicial investigation of the whole Hebrang case.

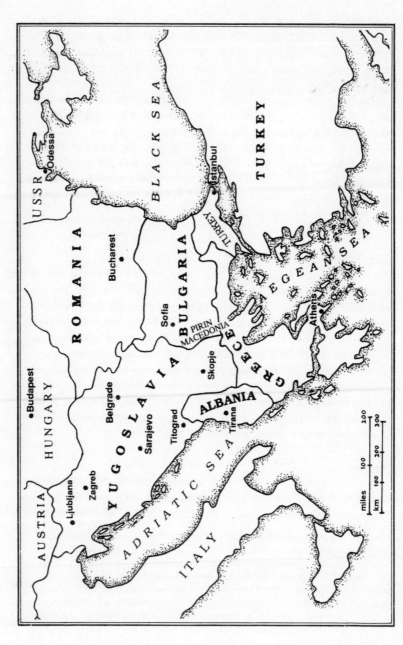

**Map 3 The Balkans since 1945**

because the country had not experienced either civil war or physical devastation as a result of wartime operations on its territory, the whole of the state apparatus was in place and, after purges in the army and the civil service, ready to serve the new masters. Second, the non-communists still feared in the immediate post-1945 period that, since Romania was a former enemy country, the Western Allies might prevent it from regaining northern Transylvania (which had been awarded by the Axis powers to Hungary in 1940). Soviet support was, therefore, seen as essential in securing this vital national objective and the communists, as Moscow's friends, were best placed to secure it. This tactic proved correct. Romania managed, with Stalin's backing, to get northern Transylvania back. This was a strong boost for the communists.

### Bulgaria

The Bulgarian Communist Party was larger than the Romanian one. In September 1944, it claimed to have some 25,000 members. Non-communists asserted that the real figure was more like 8,000 – but this was still eight times more than Romania. The Bulgarian Party, like its Romanian counterpart, was helped in the immediate postwar period by two factors. First, the non-communists believed that the closeness of party members to Moscow (notably that of people like Georgi Dimitrov, a senior Comintern figure) could help prevent the imposition on Bulgaria of heavy wartime reparations like those that had crippled its economy after World War I. This feeling was so strong that the opposition held back for patriotic reasons. Second, the communists were able to play on the Bulgarians' psychological need, understandable in a nation that had been repeatedly defeated in wars this century, for a powerful shield against a hostile world – the Soviet Union.

None of this, however, resulted in milder, more tolerant communist policies towards the Bulgarian opposition. Most prominent members of the non-communist parties were 'liquidated' within six months of the Soviet army's entry into Bulgaria in September 1944. The Bulgarian authorities instituted a purge which, per head of population, claimed more victims than in any other East European country. By March 1945, the 'people's courts' had tried 11,667 people and, of those, 2,138 were sentenced to death. Unofficial estimates put the number of victims at between 30,000 and 100,000.[8] The Bulgarian army, the strongest and best organized force that could have opposed the communists, was sent to fight alongside the Soviet army against the Germans in Hungary and Austria. By the time it came back, the communists held all the main levers of power. The army was thoroughly purged and provided with Soviet-style political commissars.

## Albania

The Albanian communists, in contrast, approached power in November 1944 in a mood of self-confidence based on the (not entirely unjustified) feeling that they had freed the country from foreign forces and defeated their domestic rivals largely by their own efforts. That self-confidence was shaken somewhat by the emergence of the Kosovo problem as a bone of contention with the powerful Yugoslav Communist Party. At the meeting of the Albanian Central Committee in November 1944, just before the communists' entry into Tirana, the capital, a Yugoslav representative attending the meeting shocked many Albanian communists by suggesting that Albania and Yugoslavia be joined in one state. The incident revealed a division within Albanian ranks, with Enver Hoxha opposed and Koci Xoxe, a powerful party figure, in favour. The plan was neither accepted nor rejected: it stayed on the agenda. The Hoxha group argued for an independent foreign policy based on friendly relations with East and West alike and, in domestic affairs, a policy of postponing radical socialist measures until agriculture and industry had advanced within the framework of a market economy. The Xoxe group pressed for immediate union and, in domestic policy, a full-blooded Bolshevik programme of social transformation similar to that embarked upon by the Yugoslav communists. This debate, resolved at first under Yugoslav pressure in the Xoxe group's favour, gave a foretaste of the full-scale conflict between Yugoslavia and Albania that was to emerge into the open in 1948.

## Yugoslavia

The Yugoslav communists displayed an even greater self-confidence when they attained power in the whole of Yugoslavia in the spring of 1945. In this euphoric mood, they ignored Soviet warnings to behave more circumspectly so as not to embarrass the Soviet Union in its relations with the Western Allies. Their cockiness was reflected in equal measure in their domestic and foreign policies. At home, the Tito regime launched an ambitious industrialization programme preceded by the fastest and most sweeping nationalization anywhere in Eastern Europe. Tito's foreign policy was even more spectacular. He challenged the Western Allies, unsuccessfully as it happened, in Austria and Trieste. In the south, Yugoslavia was the chief backer of the communist side in the Greek civil war. Tito and the Bulgarian Party leader, Georgi Dimitrov, had a plan for a South-East European Union. Behind all this lay Tito's long-term aim, clearly understood by Stalin, to form a South-East European grouping under his leadership. Stalin's realization that Tito could become a serious threat to his own hegemony in Eastern Europe was the main reason for Tito's expulsion from the Soviet bloc in 1948 after he refused to toe the line.

Tito's confidence rested to a large degree on his knowledge that his own aims were broadly in harmony with the national aims of the peoples of Yugoslavia. What these aims offered them above all was protection against traditional enemies: the Slovenes from Italy and Germany; the Croats from Italy and, even more important, from Serbia; and the Macedonians from Greece and Serbia but also from Bulgaria. What they offered the Serbs, however, was less than the total and undisputed dominance they had enjoyed in the prewar kingdom. Herein lay the seeds of the Serb backlash that followed the Tito era.

In Tito's Yugoslavia, the Serbs got a republic consisting of Serbia proper with the nominally autonomous provinces of Vojvodina in the north and, most important, Kosovo, centre of Serbia's medieval state, in the south. In addition, during the first two postwar decades, the Serbs enjoyed a dominant position in Croatia and Bosnia, despite being a minority of the population there. This dominance, which lasted right up to the dismissal in 1966 of Aleksandar Rankovic, a Serb and the powerful security chief and party cadre secretary, was due to the large preponderance of Serbs in the party, the army and the security services in those two republics. This stemmed from their massive participation in the partisan ranks in Croatia as a result of their persecution by the Pavelic regime. Many Cetniks joined the partisans after an amnesty in 1943. Tito's mobilization in Serbia in 1944 for the expulsion of the Germans and the final victory, which he wanted to achieve without Russian help, also increased the proportion of Serbs in the army.

From the party's point of view, there was something to be said for soothing the Serbs' feelings over what many of them regarded as two bitter losses. The first was that Bosnia, a key element in Serbia's national expansion programme since the middle of the nineteenth century, had not been formally joined with Serbia under the new federal arrangement, despite strenuous efforts by some Serbian communists. The Serbs regarded their informal control in Bosnia in the first two postwar decades as necessarily impermanent. This was a correct calculation, as was proved when the more numerous Muslims subsequently became the dominant group there at the end of the 1960s.

The other loss, from the point of view of the Serbian national agenda, was the 'abandonment' of Macedonia ('Old Serbia' in prewar Yugoslavia) through the granting of federal autonomy to the Macedonian Republic. This meant in effect the abandonment of landlocked Serbia's *Drang nach Saloniki*, its plan to gain access to the Aegean Sea.*

The other three communist regimes in the Balkans – the Albanian one divided and the Bulgarian and Romanian ones lacking in self-confidence – were not able to draw upon as wide a national consensus as the Tito regime. They were obliged to recognize Yugoslavia's clear regional supremacy, though not for long.

---

*The Germans played on this Serbian ambition when, in negotiations in early 1941 designed to induce the then royal Yugoslav government to join the Tripartite Pact (Germany, Italy and Japan), they promised it Greek Macedonia with the port of Salonika. This promise was recorded in a secret protocol that accompanied Yugoslavia's adherence to the Pact on 25 March 1941. The Axis connection was repudiated in a British-inspired officers' coup two days later. This brought Yugoslavia warm praise from Winston Churchill but also provoked Hitler's rage and led to Yugoslavia's annihilation at the hands of the *Wehrmacht* the following month.

# 3
# THE COLD WAR CORSET

For much of the period between the two world wars, the Great Powers displayed a policy of benign neglect towards the Balkans: the United States because of the onset of isolationism after 1919; Britain and France because they were engaged elsewhere; and the Soviet Union and Germany because they were temporarily disabled – the former by revolution and civil war, the latter by military defeat. The only European power to pursue an active policy in the area was Italy, one of the victors in 1918 but not particularly happy with its territorial gains. Against the pro-French Little Entente (Czechoslovakia, Romania and Yugoslavia), which was designed to maintain the status quo, Italy backed the anti-Versailles, 'revisionist' regimes in Austria, Bulgaria and Hungary and supported Croat groups working for Yugoslavia's disintegration (notably the Pavelic Ustasa group). This support lasted until well into the 1930s, when Italy reached an understanding with Belgrade.

The Balkans assumed greater strategic importance in the mid-1930s with the re-emergence of Germany as a serious competitor to Italy; the Soviet Union continued to operate chiefly through the local communist parties. The outbreak of war and subsequent events, including the communist takeover in Albania, Bulgaria, Romania and Yugoslavia, des-cribed in Chapter 2, accelerated the process. Soon the region had regained its pre–1914 status as an important theatre of Great Power conflict. The Western allies conceded the Soviet Union's predominance in Bulgaria and Romania, exactly as had been foreshadowed in the informal 'percentages' understanding over the division of spheres of interest reached by Churchill and Stalin in Moscow in October 1944.[9]

They lost out in Yugoslavia, where there should have been a 50:50 relationship, and in Albania, over which there had been no agreement. But the Western powers could – and did – hold their ground in Greece and Turkey. First Britain helped the non-communist Greek government defeat a communist attempt to seize power in 1944–5. Then in 1947–8, in order to contain the Soviet threat in south-eastern Europe and the Mediterranean, the United States offered military and economic assistance to both Greece and Turkey. This culminated in their membership of Nato. A major role was played in the defeat of the Greek communists after 1945 by Tito's decision after his expulsion from Cominform in 1948 to reduce his support for the Greek guerrillas and then in July 1949 his closure of the frontiers to them.

Yugoslavia's expulsion from the Soviet bloc threatened to destabilize the post-1945 Balkan alignment. But the brief period of uncertainty ended relatively quickly when the Western powers stepped in, providing Yugoslavia with military and economic aid and even a link with Nato through the Balkan Pact between Greece, Turkey and Yugoslavia, signed in February 1953. This more or less restored the 50:50 ratio, although the fact that Yugoslavia remained communist under Tito's leadership represented an important guarantee in Moscow's eyes. The stand-off over Yugoslavia between the West and the Soviet Union remained in force for more than three decades, even beyond Tito's death in 1980.

### Albania's balancing act

After the communists had taken over in Albania, the country was rapidly turned into a satellite of Yugoslavia, which in its turn was then still a satellite (though, admittedly, already an awkward one) of the Soviet Union. Albania's dependent position was reflected in the treaty of friendship, cooperation and mutual aid it signed with Yugoslavia in July 1946. The treaty envisaged the coordination of economic plans between the two countries, the standardization of their monetary systems, the creation of a customs union and the unification of prices.

To implement these policies, a large number of Yugoslav experts were sent to Albania and given key positions in government departments and the armed forces. Serbian was made a compulsory subject in Albanian schools. Joint-stock companies were set up to exploit Albania's oil and other minerals. The Albanians much resented their own unequal status, as junior partners, in these companies. (Ironically, one of the reasons for the growing resentment of the Soviet Union among Yugoslavia's own leaders was Moscow's imposition of similar bodies on them at about the same time.) Like Italy before it, Yugoslavia supplied half of Albania's budget needs.

In reality, Albania had become a vassal state on the road to full absorption into what most Albanians saw as another version of Serbia. Keeping it in that position was the job of the pro-Yugoslav faction in the leadership. This was led by Koci Xoxe, who took on the mantle of Esad Pasha, the vassal of the prewar, royalist Yugoslavia. Though a minority, the Xoxe faction, with the help of the numerous Yugoslav personnel in Albania, ensured compliance with Belgrade's wishes. Some opponents of union with Yugoslavia were purged. Nako Spiru, who was in charge of economic policy in Albania, found himself caught in an insoluble conflict of interests and committed suicide in November 1947. Mehmet Shehu, Xoxha's military strong man, was pushed out of office shortly afterwards, although he reappeared after the break with Yugoslavia in 1948.

The Tito–Stalin dispute was a godsend to Hoxha and his faction. His own survival was due to a combination of cunning and a willingness to eat humble pie – which he could afford to do when appropriate because of his dominant position within the party's and the army's wartime cadres. Hoxha and his supporters were jubilant when Yugoslavia was expelled from the Cominform (Communist Information Bureau). This had been set up in 1947, with its headquarters in Belgrade, and was supposed to act as a replacement in Europe for the Comintern, which had been disbanded in 1943 in order to reassure the Western Allies that the Soviet Union would not use the war to promote the cause of world revolution.

Albania immediately repudiated all its economic agreements with Yugoslavia on the grounds that they were incompatible with national sovereignty, and expelled all Yugoslav civilian and military advisers and other personnel. Albania became the first East European state to line up behind the Soviet Union in its campaign against Yugoslavia – a move which not only reflected the Albanian regime's hostility towards Belgrade but also its sense of insecurity from the continuing Anglo-American attempts to overthrow it. A few months later, the Soviet Union concluded an agreement with Albania under which it promised to make good the economic and technical aid Albania had forfeited because of its break with Yugoslavia.

It is easy to understand the Albanian leaders' elation. First, Yugoslavia's disgrace had, at one and the same time, removed the danger of

Albania's absorption by its bigger neighbour and given it what it had always wanted: a distant patron which had no territorial designs on it and yet was willing to protect it against not only Yugoslavia but also Greece and its Western allies – as well as giving it economic aid. Second, the Soviet–Yugoslav conflict raised Albanian hopes, later to be disappointed, that Yugoslavia might have to disgorge its Albanians and thus make possible the union of all Albanians in one state under communist leadership. Last but not least, the dispute provided Enver Hoxha with an opportunity to get rid of Koci Xoxe and other pro-Yugoslav leaders. In May 1949 Xoxe was tried in Tirana for high treason and sentenced to death.

Albania did well out of the Soviet–Yugoslav dispute. By hitching itself directly to the bigger ship, it obtained significant financial help (estimated at $600 million) from the Soviet Union for numerous projects. These included a number of hydroelectric power stations, which made an important contribution to Albania's energy supply. The Soviet naval presence in a submarine base in Vlore across the southern Adriatic from Italy was a mark of the strategic importance attached to small Albania by its distant but powerful ally.

But the Soviet–Albanian honeymoon did not survive Stalin. The Soviet–Yugoslav rapprochement, which began in 1954 and culminated in Nikita Khrushchev's visit to Belgrade in 1955 and Tito's to Moscow in 1956, was a dangerous time for Enver Hoxha. He feared, not without reason, that he and his country might be sacrificed by Khrushchev in the interests of good relations with Tito. Khrushchev wanted to harness Tito's influence in Eastern Europe for his own ends. Once more the Albanians had a last-minute escape, thanks to the outbreak of a new quarrel between Belgrade and Moscow in 1957. But they remained on their guard. Indeed, in 1960 it looked as if, yet again, Albania might be quietly abandoned by Moscow as part of a new Soviet–Yugoslav rapprochement – until the Sino-Soviet dispute presented the Albanians with a lifeline, and a new distant patron.

In the course of 1961, Soviet submarines were withdrawn from the naval base at Vlore, and Soviet and East European credits promised for 1961–5 were cancelled. China promptly stepped in and announced that it was giving Albania $125 million worth of credits – roughly what the Soviet bloc would have offered. Chinese specialists replaced those withdrawn from Albania by the Soviet Union and other East European countries. For Albania, the cost of the switch was great in material terms – its five-year plan had been geared to deliveries from the Soviet Union and Eastern Europe – but the alliance with China, the most populous country in the world, was an important boost to the Albanian regime's prestige. It was further enhanced when the Sino-Soviet dispute later erupted into a full-scale ideological conflict and small Albania became, with China, the Mecca of pure Marxist–Leninists from all over the world.

## Romania's bid for independence

The Sino-Soviet split also helped the Romanian communist regime to broaden its originally extremely narrow base of support in the country by demonstrating to the population that it was ready and able to stand up to the Soviet Union in defence of Romania's national interests. In the immediate postwar period Romania was, of all the East European countries, the most exploited by the Soviet Union. Moscow imposed heavy reparations, classifying it, along with Bulgaria and Hungary, as a former enemy country. Romania's switch to the Allied side in August 1944 did not help in this respect. Merchant ships and railway rolling stock were impounded and transported to the Soviet Union, as were large quantities of industrial and semi-manufactured goods. Even whole plants were dismantled and removed. The Soviet–Romanian joint-stock companies controlled all sectors of economic life, including crude oil, uranium, chemicals, timber and shipping. German assets seized by the Soviet authorities provided Soviet capital. Romanian exports to and imports from the Soviet Union suffered from price discrimination.

Even later on, in the second half of the 1950s and the early 1960s, when the Soviet Union started to shore up the troubled East European economies, Romania remained bottom of the list – despite the fact that it was a key supplier to the Soviet economy of oil products, uranium, timber and foodstuffs. The gap between Romania and the more advanced East European countries widened, with the prospect – at that time perceived as intolerable by the country's communists and non-communists alike – that Romania would remain the lowly supplier of food and raw materials to the industrialized parts of the Soviet bloc. The tight Soviet grip on the Romanian economy reinforced the already strong anti-Soviet feeling among the population. More important, the knowledge that Romania was being discriminated against in comparison with the other East European countries caused intense frustration to many in the Romanian *nomenklatura* (ruling group).

Stalin's death left Romania's hardline and deeply unpopular leadership in an exposed position. Its sense of vulnerability increased with the onset of the de-Stalinization campaign in the Soviet bloc in the wake of Khrushchev's speech denouncing Stalin in February 1956. Two other events in the autumn of 1956 made the Romanian leaders even more nervous: the political upheaval in Poland and, even more, the outbreak of the Hungarian revolution, with its political echoes among the Hungarian population in Transylvania. The withdrawal in 1958 of Soviet troops, which had been stationed in Romania since 1944, provoked further reappraisal. Though unpopular with the people as a symbol of Soviet dominance, these troops had represented to the Romanian regime – as they had to others in Eastern Europe – an important political guarantee. Something else was needed to replace it. The time had come to play the nationalist card.

It was no accident that Romania started to play that card when it did – in 1960–61. The time was right. First of all, the Sino-Soviet split gave the Romanian leadership unexpected room for manoeuvre – just as it did the Albanians. At that moment, anybody opposing Moscow in the Soviet bloc was exceptionally safe. For Moscow, disciplining recalcitrant satellites like Romania would have meant diverting attention and energy from the far more urgent task of responding to China's difficult challenge.

Secondly, the ruling group was united behind the party leader, Gheorge Gheorghiu-Dej, a 'home communist' who had spent the 1933–44 period in Romanian gaols. It had an attractive cause – Romania's modernization and industrialization – that appealed both to the party elite and to the ordinary people. Gheorghiu-Dej and his colleagues, notably Nicolae Ceausescu, who was to succeed him on his death in 1965, simply broadened this into a direct appeal to Romanian nationalism in every other sphere. They were quite consciously playing on feelings which some of them had in any case quietly shared with their fellow-Romanians, above all the view of Romania as a rather superior island of Latinity surrounded by a Slav sea.

That is why the new, more openly nationalist policy had a strong cultural content. Quite apart from separating the Romanians neatly from the Slavs and the Hungarians, more immediate tactical benefits could be gained from the renewed publicity and emphasis given to Romanian national history. It was obviously politically useful to the regime in a country where aversion to Russia ran deep to be able to draw parallels between the resistance to the Romans of the Dacians (from whom modern Romanians claim descent) and contemporary resistance to Soviet domination. Invariably, the Romanian public responded patriotically, which was extremely gratifying to the regime.

Although the stress in the 1960s and the 1970s may have been on anti-Russianism, it was kept within very careful limits. This was to avoid a head-on challenge to Moscow on any important issue, not least over Bessarabia, which had become the Moldavian Soviet Republic after 1945. The Romanian regime never once formally raised the issue with Moscow until Ceausescu's downfall in December 1989. Even when, under Mikhail Gorbachev, public unrest in Moldavia came out into the open, with demands for help from Romania, the Ceausescu regime studiously ignored such demands.

From Moscow's point of view, an independent Romanian foreign policy was actually never considered a serious threat. Surrounded by communist states, Romania was in no position – even if it wanted to – to declare itself neutral, let alone switch alliances. As for establishing a multi-party political system, Moscow knew very well that that was the last thing Romania's Stalinist leadership was interested in. In fact, it relied on the Soviet connection as the ultimate guarantee of its own domestic monopoly of power. But for all that, Moscow was not prepared simply to tolerate certain Romanian foreign policy initiatives and wanted to warn the country's leaders not to overstep the limit.

A conduit was to hand for conveying such warnings: Hungary, a faithful follower of the Soviet foreign policy line ever since the communists took full power there in 1948.* The chosen method of warning Romania off was Soviet-approved Hungarian criticism of Romania's nationality policy.

One warning came in the wake of the Soviet-led Warsaw Pact invasion of Czechoslovakia in August 1968, which Romania had refused to take part in and publicly condemned. A senior Hungarian Politburo member, who was also the party's main specialist on nationality issues, travelled to Bucharest within a few days of Czechoslovakia's invasion and raised with the Romanian leaders the subject of the Hungarians' position in Transylvania.

Another warning was issued in 1971 when the Soviet leadership was worried by the possibility that China might be in the process of establishing a sphere of influence in the Balkans. There was some justification for these fears: Romania's relations with China had become close; those between Yugoslavia and China were improving after a long period of strain; and Albania, then still China's ally, was moving closer both to

---

*There was, of course, a brief exception between October and early November 1956 under the multi-party government of Imre Nagy, which was swiftly overthrown by direct Soviet military intervention.

Romania and to Yugoslavia. In June 1971, a senior Hungarian Politburo member referred publicly to the position of the Hungarian minority in Romania as a cause of difficulties in relations between the two countries. Later that summer, a Budapest newspaper praised the settlement between Italy and Austria over the German-speaking minority in the Italian region of Alto Adige (South Tyrol) in a way which made the parallel between Transylvania and the Tyrol quite clear.

By way of response, Romanian historians, with plenty of official encouragement, stepped up their efforts to prove that Transylvania had, ever since Roman times, been under continuous occupation, first by the Dacians, then by their direct descendants. The Hungarians' argument was that, on the contrary, during the Dark Ages and Early Middle Ages Transylvania had become 'empty' – to be settled later by the Hungarians, the Germans and, of course, also the Romanians, staying under (direct or indirect) Hungarian rule until 1918. The Romanian defensiveness was not based on a fear that Hungary, a country half Romania's size, could realistically hope to take Transylvania back by its own efforts. For the status quo to be altered in its favour, Hungary would need a powerful ally or allies, as it did in 1940 when it acquired northern Transylvania with backing from Hitler and Mussolini. In postwar Eastern Europe, this ally could only be the Soviet Union. But Moscow, mindful of the need to avoid bringing into question Soviet post-1945 territorial conquests, carefully refrained from doing anything that could, however indirectly, upset the territorial status quo in Eastern Europe. Clearly, though, this did not stop the Soviet leaders making tactical use of temporarily dormant territorial disputes as a means of putting pressure on their smaller allies.

With increasing liberalization in Hungary, the issue of Transylvania began to slip out of the control of the authorities in Budapest and was gradually taken over in the late 1970s and the early 1980s by the opposition movement. Espousing the cause of the Hungarians in Transylvania was useful to the opposition because it broadened its base of support, by combining the inevitably less popular concern for human rights and civil liberties with a far wider patriotic appeal.

These developments worried the Ceausescu regime, whose prestige abroad was harmed by the unfavourable international attention being drawn to its repression of the Hungarian minority at home. It was perhaps even more urgently concerned about the effect the renewed public Hungarian interest in Transylvania might have on Romania's Hungarians. It responded by deliberately fostering an old-style chauvinism, with a particularly strong anti-Hungarian edge to it, through various government-supported organizations.*

## Bulgaria's uneasy course

The regime in Bulgaria, as in Albania, had to swallow a bitter pill in the immediate aftermath of World War II. Putting up with the position of junior partner vis-à-vis the Tito regime in Yugoslavia was particularly galling for Bulgarian communists because of their party's longer revolutionary pedigree and the fact that it was headed by one of the most senior figures of the world communist movement. Georgi Dimitrov had achieved world-wide fame in 1934 by his defiance at the trial staged by the Nazis in order to implicate the communists in the fire that had destroyed the Reichstag building in Berlin shortly after Hitler came to power. Nevertheless, Bulgaria's communist partisans never numbered more than 10,000 to 15,000 men, whereas Tito enjoyed the glamour of a successful revolutionary leader whose partisan movement could boast of having achieved power by its own efforts.

### The Macedonian muddle

Bulgaria's junior position involved, above all, accepting the incorporation of Macedonia into Yugoslavia as one of its federal republics. In the nineteenth century, there was widespread agreement among European scholars that the Slav inhabitants of Macedonia were Bulgarians. However, the Serbs, who had achieved autonomy from the Ottoman empire in 1829 and had plans to expand their territory southwards, westwards and northwards, claimed Macedonia right down to Salonika on ethnic grounds, asserting that its Slav inhabitants were Serbs. The Greeks, who had achieved their independence in 1832 and had plans to expand northwards, based their claim to Macedonia on both historical and ethnic grounds. The Treaty of San Stefano in 1878, concluded at the end of the

*Even after the downfall of the Ceausescu regime in 1989, the tactic is still being used. In the immediate aftermath of Ceausescu's fall, a body called Vatra Romaneasca (Romanian Hearth) was established with help from certain old party strata. It was dedicated to the 'patriotic education' of the Romanian masses, and has continued to play a prominent role in spreading anti-Hungarian propaganda among the population.

Russo–Turkish war, had given the newly independent Bulgaria the whole of Macedonia. But later that year it was returned to Turkey, following the nullification of the treaty at the Berlin Congress. This was at the joint insistence of Britain and Austria–Hungary, neither of which was willing to contemplate a new state beholden to Russia reaching as far as the Aegean. Restoration of the San Stefano borders became Bulgaria's national goal.

Rivalry between Bulgaria, Greece and Serbia over Macedonia, a Balkan no man's land – accompanied by fighting among armed irregulars of all nationalities – remained one of the central issues of Balkan politics for the following two decades. In 1912 the three Christian Balkan countries decided to sink their differences. Together with tiny Montenegro, they formed the Balkan League, which immediately declared war on Turkey, hoping to benefit from its involvement in a war with Italy. Turkey was overwhelmingly defeated. The victors fell out over the division of the spoils and a new war broke out, with Bulgaria on one side and Greece, Montenegro, Romania and Serbia on the other. Bulgaria lost and sought to avenge itself by siding with the Central Powers during World War I. Having found itself on the losing side, Bulgaria ended with only the small region of Pirin Macedonia. The bulk of Macedonia was divided between Greece and the new Yugoslavia, Serbia's successor-state.

Bulgaria's brief period of triumph in World War II included the recapture of Yugoslav Macedonia and, in 1941, the occupation of Thrace in Greece. But in 1944 Bulgaria was obliged to hand back the portion of Macedonia it had taken away from Yugoslavia, once again retaining only Pirin Macedonia. In addition it was forced to hand back to Greece not only Thrace but also Greek Macedonia, which the Germans had allowed it to occupy as well. Bulgaria's brutal occupation of Thrace left behind a legacy of bitterness.

In 1944, Bulgarian and Yugoslav communists agreed to recognize the existence of a separate Macedonian nationality. They did so, however, with completely opposite motives. The Tito regime, whose foreign policy goals were nothing if not ambitious, saw the recognition of Macedonian nationality as a step towards the eventual unification of all Macedonians, including those in Bulgaria and Greece, under Yugoslav leadership. In the shorter term, the Tito regime hoped that the Macedonians' recognition as a nation on a par with the Serbs, the Croats and other fully-fledged Yugoslav nations would help to bind them more closely to Yugoslavia, from which they had been alienated by the pre-1941

Serbianization policy. By the same token, Belgrade hoped that the recognition of a separate Macedonian nationality would also undermine Bulgaria's claim, as well as loosening still further Macedonia's connection with Bulgaria. This had already been weakened by the indifferent treatment it had received under Bulgarian rule from 1941 to 1944.

For their part, the Bulgarian communists realized that in the wake of defeat Bulgaria was in no position to renew and actively pursue its claim on Macedonia. On the other hand, they hoped that the recognition of a separate Macedonian nationality would, for the time being at any rate, serve as an obstacle to further assimilation by the Greeks and the Serbs. The unspoken hope here was that Macedonia, because of its historical and ethnic links, would continue to gravitate towards Bulgaria and, in the fullness of time, perhaps even reunite with it formally. Since a Macedonian Republic could achieve unification with Bulgaria more easily within a common framework that included Yugoslavia in a Balkan Federation, the Bulgarian communists were in favour of the Federation when it was revived in 1944. From 1944 to 1948 the Bulgarian Communist Party even officially supported the idea of the secession of Pirin Macedonia to a Macedonian Socialist Federal Republic within the future Balkan Federation. However, in 1948 Stalin vetoed the project for such a federation.

Yugoslavia's expulsion from the Cominform in June 1948 came as a relief to Bulgaria. It released it from the embarrassing commitment to give up Bulgarian territory. The Bulgarian regime continued to recognize the Macedonian nationality, not least in order to keep its own Macedonians loyal in the political and propaganda conflict with Yugoslavia. But links with Yugoslav Macedonia were severed. After Georgi Dimitrov's death in July 1949 (both his parents came from Macedonia), the policy began to change. First, the regime declared that the process of forming a separate Macedonian nationality had begun only in 1918. Later the date was moved to 1944. In April 1956, the Bulgarian Party decided at a plenary meeting of its Central Committee to withdraw its recognition of the existence of a separate Macedonian nationality. This was done as a concession to rising Bulgarian nationalism. Despite this important change in policy, the next census, held in December 1956, still provided an entry for a separate Macedonian nationality and showed that there were 187,789 'Macedonians' in Bulgaria. It was only in 1960 that the official Bulgarian statistical yearbook ceased to show a separate entry for the Macedonians. The first renewed Bulgarian claims to Macedonia appeared in a discreet form in 1958 in connection with the eightieth anniversary of the San Stefano Treaty. But the Bulgarian claims always carefully referred to Macedonia's 'Bulgarian past', coupled with statements affirming the political status quo.

Yugoslavia responded very promptly the same year, setting up, under its own Metropolitan, a separate Macedonian Orthodox church. This was indeed unusual – an atheist communist regime actually helping to set up a church – but it was not unprecedented. After all, in 1943 Stalin had reconstituted the virtually extinct Russian Orthodox hierarchy his regime had all but destroyed, because he badly needed the bishops to call on the Russian masses to fight for 'holy Russia'. The people had already shown, by surrendering *en masse* to the Germans in the early days of the war, that they were reluctant to die for Stalin and communism. Yugoslavia had made a shrewd political move with regard to the Macedonian church. In an Orthodox setting, an autocephalous church is one of the highest attributes of nationhood. To soothe Serb feelings (the Macedonian Orthodox had, ever since Serbia acquired Macedonia in 1913, been under the jurisdiction of the Serbian Patriarch), the newly established church decided to remain in canonical unity with the Serbian Orthodox church.

With these moves Yugoslavia consolidated its hold on Macedonia. Particularly upsetting for Bulgaria was the Soviet Union's apparent acquiescence, which turned into something even worse from the Bulgarian point of view. In 1962, Patriarch Alexis of Moscow, head of the Russian Orthodox church, visited Skopje, the capital of the Yugoslav Republic of Macedonia, and met the Macedonian Archbishop. In view of the close control exercised over the Russian Orthodox church by the Soviet authorities, there could hardly have been a clearer way of demonstrating Soviet recognition of the Macedonian nationality. In 1967, the Macedonian Archbishop was upgraded to Patriarch. The outraged Serbian Orthodox bishops wanted to anathematize not only the Macedonians concerned but also all Yugoslav officials who had a hand in the matter. A head-on and politically damaging clash with Serbian nationalism, which the Serbian Orthodox church embodied, was narrowly averted by pressure on the Serbian Patriarch, a pliable man close to the authorities.

## The patriotic campaign

As long as the Soviet–Yugoslav rapprochement continued, Bulgaria had to behave circumspectly over national questions. Its moment came with the invasion of Czechoslovakia in 1968, to which Bulgaria made a token contribution but which Yugoslavia condemned. At Soviet behest, as part of a damage-limitation campaign, the government issued an official statement in September that Bulgaria 'has not had and does not have territorial ambitions with regard to any country' and that it accepted 'the inviolability of the frontiers established after World War II'. It also emphasized its wish for good relations with Yugoslavia. But this whole episode enabled the regime to expand the propaganda campaign that had begun in a low key in 1967 and that aimed to identify the party with Bulgarian patriotism.

This campaign had followed an abortive coup in April 1965, led by a group of nationalist-minded senior Bulgarian army officers unhappy with the regime's humiliating subservience to Moscow, which had demonstrated the weakness of the party and its leader, Todor Zhivkov. The Bulgarian regime lost much support after turning away from economic reform in 1968. Its unpopularity increased in the 1970s as economic growth failed to produce any political relaxation and Zhivkov continued to pursue a slavishly pro-Soviet line.

Meanwhile, Bulgaria's image abroad continued to be blackened by a series of scandals like the 'poisoned umbrella tip' case in 1978, involving the murder in London of the well-known Bulgarian dissident, Georgi Markov, by an unknown assailant suspected of being a Bulgarian agent; and the assassination attempt on Pope John II, also widely attributed to Bulgaria's secret service. The regime was also worried about its unpopularity with the young, among whom the appeal of Western culture and ideas was growing. The culmination of the 'patriotic' campaign was reached in the grandiose programme of celebrations in 1981 to mark 1,300 years of Bulgarian statehood. The driving force behind the celebrations was Zhivkov's daughter, Lyudmila, the country's cultural overlord. Heavy emphasis during the anniversary events on the fact that Bulgaria was the first Slav nation to achieve its statehood – even before Russia itself – caused some displeasure in Moscow. Indeed, many in Bulgaria believed the widespread rumour that Lyudmila's sudden death had not been from natural causes but the work of Soviet agents.

## The communist failure

As the examples quoted above demonstrate, Balkan communist regimes, far from 'solving' the national question, as they had proudly claimed, dealt with it even less successfully than their 'bourgeois' predecessors had done. Like them, they derived important political advantages from their manipulation of nationalism at home and in relations with other countries. But the very nationalism the communists had appropriated and had come to rely upon to help keep them in power blew up in their face in the end. In the late 1980s their own people turned on them in the name of the very same patriotism that they had been preaching. Ironically, they were found wanting not so much as communists but as the patriots they professed to be. The bill for the communists' failures in this as in other fields, however, is now being paid by their successors.

Looking back on events in the Balkans since 1945, it is no exaggeration to say that under communist rule national conflicts within the individual Balkan countries and between them have both widened and sharpened, even where – as in Yugoslavia – an attempt was made to tackle problems in a more fundamental way. One of the greatest indictments of the communist regimes in the Balkans was their failure to protect the linguistic and cultural diversity in the territories under their jurisdiction.*

The reasons for this failure have to be sought in communism's suppression of open and free debate about controversial issues and hence of free representation of interests. Without independent public criticism, the imposition from above (not always from unworthy motives) of 'official', carefully sanitized versions of past and present disputes only increased public cynicism and disbelief. This in turn encouraged, or at any rate did nothing to prevent or neutralize, the growth of prejudice and hatred, which threatened to fuel violent explosions in the future. What paved the way for those explosions, and thus also the collapse of the system itself, was communism's failure to live up to its economic promises.

---

*Yugoslavia's record was quite good here: tolerance was shown for minorities such as the Hungarians, the Albanians (from 1968 to 1988-9), and even the gypsies; but there was a harsh response to the Croat demand for the right to separate language status.

# 4

# THE ECONOMIC BLACK HOLE

When the map of Europe was redrawn after World War II, south-eastern Europe came to be divided into economic zones that were exactly co-terminous with its political divisions. Albania, Bulgaria, Romania and Yugoslavia had the Soviet type of command economic systems imposed on them by their new rulers. Greece and Turkey, in the Western political sphere, remained market economies, although with a strong public sector.

The pre-communist era had been by no means prosperous, let alone trouble-free for the countries of this region. In the period between 1918 and 1941, their already serious economic disadvantages were aggravated by the fact that their numerous political troubles spilled over everywhere into the economy. As a result of conflicts between the new states that had come into being after 1918, customs barriers went up, cutting across prewar trade routes. In the 1930s the depression caused much devastation. All that the Balkans had by way of industry were some consumer-goods industries and some engineering factories in certain areas. About four-fifths of the population earned their living from agriculture. The whole region suffered from shortages of domestic capital and skilled labour.

The potential for industrialization did exist: the region had plentiful natural resources, except for energy. There were rich (though unevenly distributed) deposits of non-ferrous metals, including copper, chrome, lead and zinc in Albania, Bulgaria, Greece and Turkey, as well as in Yugoslavia, which also had plenty of bauxite. There were large oil-fields in Romania, as well as some oil in Albania. There was plenty of lignite but hardly any coal or good-quality iron ore. Timber was plentiful, but the poor infrastructure and lack of capital hampered the production of other agricultural raw materials.

After 1918 all the Balkan states pursued a policy of industrialization behind high tariff barriers designed to protect domestic industry. This completed the destruction of the old Danubian economic region, the economic counterpart of the Austro–Hungarian empire. Regional customs unions were a non-starter for political reasons, mainly connected with fear of domination by the old financial centres of Vienna and Budapest. Most of the badly needed foreign capital was used for resettling refugees, stabilizing currencies, modernizing production and infrastructure, buying arms and maintaining large public-sector bureaucracies Heavy indebtedness ended in moratoriums for Bulgaria, Greece, Romania, Turkey and Yugoslavia.

The rapid decline of agricultural prices hit these countries extremely hard. Their main trading partners imposed restrictions on agricultural imports. Closer cooperation among the countries of the area was not feasible for political reasons but also because of their lack of economic complementarity. The introduction of foreign-exchange controls meant that an ever greater proportion of trade with their main partners had to be conducted through bilateral clearing accounts.

## The communist economic model

When the communists took over after World War II, they nationalized industry, mining, trade, banking and insurance. But the pace at which they did so varied considerably. Bulgaria and Romania were classified as former enemy countries and subject to a degree of supervision by Allied Control Commissions – at least until the conclusion of the peace treaties in 1946–7. As part of the coalition of victorious powers, Yugoslavia and its then client-state, Albania, were free from those external restraints. In addition they were led by self-confident leaders, flushed with their revolutionary victory. So, not surprisingly, they were the first in the field, in 1946–7, with a comprehensive nationalization that took in everything down to the smallest village shop.

Over the collectivization of agriculture, too, there was a difference of pace. Again, Yugoslavia was the radical. It embarked on the project in 1949, before Bulgaria, for example, although Bulgaria was in many ways better prepared thanks to its old and well-developed cooperative tradition in agriculture and, particularly, the existence of a state marketing agency (*Hranoiznos*), founded in the pre-communist era.

This time, however, Albania did not follow suit. The two countries' economic as well as political paths had begun to diverge sharply since the Stalin–Tito quarrel had come out into the open the year before. Albania had been intending to collectivize but was forced to wait because of the peasants' bitter resistance amid a desperate economic crisis, itself partly brought on by the break with Yugoslavia. There was an acute shortage of food in Albania. In the immediate postwar years, the country had come to rely on Yugoslavia to provide it with grain and other foodstuffs in times of bad harvests. To prevent Albania from collapsing altogether, food and other supplies were sent by air from Bulgaria and Hungary, by Soviet ships through the Dardanelles or by rail across Austria to Trieste, then under Western military government, and from there by sea to Albanian ports.

## The politics of collectivization

It was political considerations that spurred Yugoslav leaders on to collectivize so soon, despite the fact that their economy too was in very poor shape. They needed to demonstrate to many of their own supporters at home that their communist orthodoxy, impugned by Soviet-bloc critics, was still intact. Unlike the other three communist-ruled Balkan states, Yugoslavia de-collectivized in 1953, after a disastrous drop in agricultural output brought on by strong passive resistance by the peasantry. But the decision to de-collectivize was preceded by a long struggle within the regime. It was necessary to overcome strong opposition from local agro-bureaucracies afraid of losing their power and jobs. Many other communists (including some in the Politburo) had been worried that 'creeping capitalism' in the countryside might lead to its restoration elsewhere.In the end, the opponents of de-collectivization lost, but not before they had exacted their revenge: the so-called 'agrarian maximum', the upper limit on private land ownership, was set very low – at 10 hectares. This decision was to handicap Yugoslav agriculture and indeed the whole economy for many years to come.

Even in the immediate post-1918 period, the heyday of liberal capitalism in south-eastern Europe, the state's presence was felt everywhere in the Balkan economies, though not always for the best. Corruption was endemic, particularly in Romania and Yugoslavia where inadequate, poorly paid bureaucracies, inherited from prewar Romania and Serbia, suddenly found themselves with large (and much richer) new territories to administer. Not surprisingly, financial scandals abounded. State intervention in the economy increased during the slump of the 1930s.

The economies of Bulgaria and Romania survived World War II in pretty good shape. In contrast, those of Yugoslavia and Albania were devastated. But all four communist-ruled Balkan countries embarked upon ambitious programmes of rapid industrialization. They were based on swift, extensive exploitation of natural resources (including the manpower 'released' from the countryside as a result of collectivization), state investment and forced savings achieved at the expense of living standards. Growth rates of communist countries soared and soon exceeded those of Greece and Turkey, which were pursuing a policy of liberalization and deregulation with financial and technical assistance from the West.

## Pressure for reform

Very soon, however, the combination of poor living conditions, shortages of consumer goods and political repression led to social unrest. The central planning system itself, operating on the basis of fixed prices and state monopolies, wasted resources. By the late 1950s, the communist countries of south-eastern Europe were experiencing their first economic crisis in the shape of declining growth rates. By that time, the Soviet Union had taken the bulk of its war reparations from Bulgaria and Romania. It had also revised its pricing policy in trade with the East European countries, which had criticized it as unfair.

It was then that Bulgaria and Romania (though not Albania) embarked on their first cautious economic reforms and tried to expand their trade with the capitalist West. But neither task was easy: the former because of the limited nature of the economic reform exercise within an unreformed political environment; and the latter because, in contrast to Greece and Turkey, which had been relatively rapidly reintegrated into the world economy after World War II, the communist-ruled states had been absorbed into the Soviet economic sphere, at the expense of their former close trade and financial relations with the countries of Central and Western Europe.*

Autarky had been the main principle of Soviet-bloc policy, with only as much foreign trade – particularly with the capitalist West – as was

---

*In the first decade after World War I Austria, Czechoslovakia, Germany, Italy and France had been the Balkan countries' most important export markets. But by the mid-1930s Germany had outstripped them all and become the predominant trade partner throughout the whole region, a position it retained until 1945.

absolutely necessary. Western Europe and the United States made their own contribution to the widening gulf between the two Europes by operating strategic trade embargoes against the East, often a convenient excuse for keeping those countries' goods out of Western markets. The Soviet Union provided its partners with energy and a wide range of raw materials in exchange for manufactured goods produced by their recently built industries. East European (including Balkan) economies were linked to the Soviet economy through bilateral trade protocols and treaties. In addition, the Council for Mutual Economic Assistance (CMEA), popularly known in the West as Comecon, was established in 1949 but originally lacked any clearly defined role. But in 1962 the Soviet Union tried to develop it into a body fostering the Soviet bloc's integration through the coordination of economic and trade plans.

Even though such integration remained mostly on paper, membership of the Soviet bloc proved a serious handicap when, in the late 1950s, autarky was abandoned and Bulgaria, Romania and other East and Central European states found themselves obliged to try to expand their technological and trade cooperation with the West. For political reasons, Western embargoes imposed on trade with the Soviet Union applied to them too. The disastrous effects of their isolation within the communist-bloc ghetto were already very clear. They were seriously hampered by their limited export potential and the low quality of their industrial goods, attuned to the requirements of the 'soft' but apparently insatiable Soviet market rather than those of the extremely demanding world market. Though outside Comecon, Albania and Yugoslavia faced many of the same difficulties. All four Balkan states chose different approaches to deal with their problems. These will be examined in greater detail in the following sections, but can be summarized briefly as follows:

*Bulgaria* tried its luck in world (especially Middle Eastern and Mediterranean) markets, but never allowed any loosening of its extremely close Soviet connection. For a time this policy seemed to pay off, but by the end of the 1980s when the Soviet connection snapped, Bulgaria was in a critical economic condition, and an environmental ruin to boot.

The far better endowed *Romania* chose the path of economic independence, hoping to build a modern, competitive economy by relying on its good connections with both the West and the developing world. It ended up by squandering its oil assets; moreover, the regime's insistence during the 1980s on avoiding external credit at all costs while also paying off all existing debts resulted in a dramatic decline in living standards throughout Romanian society and had a disastrous effect on its infrastructure, which came to be totally neglected.

*Albania* was a member of Comecon from 1949 to 1962. *Yugoslavia* became an observer member in 1956. But they had other connections too. Foreign assistance on a large scale was the crucial factor for both. But it was not an unmixed blessing. Given for political reasons, that assistance – to Albania by Russia and then China, and to Yugoslavia by the West – certainly helped those countries' regimes to survive. It is no exaggeration to say that, without that tangible external backing, they would very probably have gone under. But the experiment ended badly for both countries.

In the case of Albania this was because its Stalinist leaders, though ready to change foreign partners, never even for a moment considered giving up strict centralized control. Not surprisingly, the country was in a deep crisis well before Enver Hoxha's death in 1985.

Yugoslavia came unstuck because after embarking on what were then radical reforms, it quickly went back on them. Unfortunately, extensive Western aid in the early days and even more extensive Western lending in the 1970s enabled it to live way above its means for a long time before experiencing any discomfort. By the time the pains started, it was too late – the disease had gone too far and cut too deep. In short, the cushion of Western aid, provided to shore up Yugoslavia against Soviet influence, proved to be a disservice to Yugoslavia in the longer term because it deprived it of any incentive to reform in time.

## Bulgaria

Bulgaria, after managing high average annual growth rates during the early 1970s, found itself in the midst of a serious economic crisis by the end of the decade. Growth rates dropped to an average of 3.7% between 1981 and 1985. The lowest point for that period – 1.8% – was reached in 1985. In 1987 industrial output dropped to 0.7%. It was openly admitted that the crisis stemmed from such things as wasteful use of raw materials, slow technical progress and lack of skilled labour. Bulgaria had failed to achieve its planned high rate of growth in exports to the West, which in turn would have helped it overcome some of those problems.

In 1979 the so-called New Economic Mechanism was introduced – a rather timid version of the Hungarian reform programme of the same name. In the Bulgarian programme, the implementation was to be very gradual and the party's central guiding role in the economy, as in other spheres of life, was not questioned or restricted in any way. The main point of the reform package was to relieve the enterprises of irksome and inefficient compulsory plan directives and to focus instead on 'economic regulators' such as prices, profits and taxes. But the whole project, despite the great publicity given to it, remained a dead letter. At the Party Congress in 1986 there was a call for a switch from direct to indirect planning, but at the same time the party rejected the idea of market socialism. The plan's directives were eventually replaced by state orders. However, for most commodities central price setting was retained. The Congress postponed the price reform until the 1990s.

This foot-dragging over economic reforms reflected strong resistance from the state and party apparat as well as enterprise managers themselves. Chudomir Aleksandrov, the most prominent Politburo reformer, was dropped in July 1988. Meanwhile, the regime went in for meaningless gestures such as sales of industrial shares to workers to give them, it was hoped, a more direct interest in the performance of their enterprises. The regime's answer to the new troubles in the economy was an ever greater reliance on Comecon, whose share of Bulgaria's trade after 1986 exceeded 80%. The Soviet Union's share of Bulgaria's exports and imports continued at 54% throughout the 1980s.

To Bulgaria, the Soviet connection had been of enormous importance from the start. Its rapid industrialization after 1945 was carried out with Soviet technical and financial aid. Most of Bulgaria's machinery came from the Soviet Union, which also delivered many hundreds of plants in all sectors of industry, for instance, the Kremikovtsi and Lenin steelworks, the petrochemical complex near Burgas on the Black Sea coast and the Kozlodui nuclear power station. Over two-thirds of Bulgaria's total energy demand have over the years been met by the Soviet Union, with more than 90% of Bulgarian oil imports coming from there. There has been a similar degree of dependence on Soviet iron ore, pig iron and cellulose. Bulgaria managed to avoid the worst consequences of the world oil price shocks in 1973–4 and 1979–80 by buying oil from the Soviet Union at prices considerably below those on the world markets. In the 1970s, because Bulgaria could not provide enough exports to balance the value of its energy imports from there, its Soviet partner supplied generous credits. Like the other Balkan states, Bulgaria had in the Soviet Union a patron prepared to subsidize it for political reasons – just as the West aided Yugoslavia and made important concessions to Romania. By the same token, Albania had a succession of political patrons – first Yugoslavia, then the Soviet Union and finally China.

But Bulgaria paid a price for its dependence on the Soviet market.

Most Bulgarian goods could not be sold on world markets because production was geared to lower Soviet standards, and Bulgaria had lost any incentive to try to improve its competitiveness. In 1985, shortly after Gorbachev came to power, the inefficiency of the Bulgarian economy and the low quality of Bulgarian goods were for the first time openly criticized in the Soviet media. By then, Bulgaria had amassed huge deficits in its bilateral clearing with the Soviet Union.

Desperate attempts to achieve better results in industry by hasty, ill-prepared reorganizations only aggravated the crisis. The industrial output growth rate fell to 0.7% in 1987 and below zero later. Bad harvests in 1985, 1987 and 1988 were one of the principal causes of annual hard-currency deficits which led to an increase in foreign indebtedness from $1.5 billion in 1985 to $6.5 billion in 1988. Another cause of the mounting debt in the latter part of the 1980s was continual spending on prestigious projects – especially palaces built almost exclusively with Western materials. Debt-service claimed 40% of Bulgaria's hard-currency earnings. Towards the end of the decade Bulgaria was badly hit by a reduction in Soviet oil deliveries, which caused a severe energy shortage and disruption in industrial output in 1990 and early 1991.

More trouble was in store. In the late 1980s acute environmental problems created by Bulgaria's forced postwar industrialization became an important subject of public debate and, as the ecological movement gathered momentum, eventually also one of the causes of the communist regime's downfall. The process started in 1987–8 in the Danubian city of Ruse, which had become heavily polluted by chlorine gas emitted by a Romanian metallurgical plant on the other side of the river. An exhibition showing the high incidence of lung disease in Ruse over many years was mounted at the end of 1987 by an ecological group, acting with the support of the local party in Ruse but in defiance of the central authorities, which had been playing down the scale of the problem. The party admitted at first that an ecological problem existed but then took fright amid signs of mounting dissent in other spheres and broke up the ecological group.

But agitation continued. In March 1989 some former members of the Ruse group started a movement called Ecoglasnost. Its activities combined criticism of specific unpopular projects, such as plans to divert the waters of the river Mesta and to process nuclear waste in Bulgaria, with the general argument that there could be no ecological security without a proper public discussion of, and full democratic control over, all policies affecting the environment.

Suddenly, the regime found itself under fire from an unexpected direction, being blamed, for example, for breaking its own anti-pollution regulations. In all this, there was a strong undertone of patriotic anger directed against the communists as nature despoilers. It was no accident that ecology was what finally mobilized dissent in Bulgaria. The Bulgarians, rather like the Germans, are 'green' people devoted to their beautiful countryside, the source of much fierce pride. The communists, who had so assiduously beaten the patriotic drum, were found wanting precisely as patriots.

## Albania

Albania, like Bulgaria, has been helped by foreign economic assistance provided by not one but two patrons: the Soviet Union until 1961 and then China until the break between the two regimes in 1977–8. But unlike the resource-poor Bulgaria, Albania has been self-sufficient throughout the postwar period for most of its raw material needs. Minerals and related products have accounted for three-quarters of its total exports. Albania boasts of producing 23 minerals commercially, but in reality everything except the production of chrome, copper, nickel and oil is uneconomic by market criteria if labour and other costs are properly calculated. Wages in the mines are low, and forced labour was in use until recently.

Oil is Albania's oldest industry: bitumen mining had flourished even under the Romans. The modern oil industry dates back to World War I. The Italian army, then occupying a large part of southern Albania, discovered oil deposits in several areas. Italy controlled Albania's oil industry during the interwar period and intensified production there under its occupation during World War II.

After the war, the industry was managed by a joint Albanian–Yugoslav concern. But because of the lack of investment and technical expertise, by 1948 output had dropped to one-fifth of what it had been six years before. After the break with Tito, the Soviet Union stepped in and provided the necessary finance and technical skills. But towards the end of the 1950s, as relations began to worsen, the Soviet Union refused to finance investment in Albania's oil industry on the grounds that it would be a waste of money, especially as the Soviet Union was beginning to prepare for the role of world exporter of oil. Moscow advised the Albanians to concentrate instead on producing vegetables, fruit and plants for industrial use within the framework of the 'international division of

labour' in the Soviet bloc. The Chinese took a different view and supported the oil industry's expansion plans, with the result that production
of crude oil rose steadily to the figure of 2.7m tons in 1975. Needless to
say, the break with China in 1978 hit the industry badly.

Chrome, an essential ingredient in the production of stainless steel,
has made the most significant contribution to Albania's economy. Since
the late 1970s Albania has been the world's third largest producer of
chrome. Its fourteen mines, clustered along the Yugoslav border, have
supplied about 10% of the total world output. It has been able to produce
chrome (with nickel and cobalt as by-products) relatively cheaply,
thanks to the ample supply of power from the hydroelectric stations
begun by the Italians during World War II and then completed by the
communist regime with Soviet assistance.

After the break with the Soviet Union in 1961, China stepped in – not
least because it needed an alternative source of chrome previously pur-
chased from the Soviet Union – and financed the building of new power
stations. This allowed a rapid increase in the production of chrome and
copper. A copper wire and cable factory was built in Shkoder in the
north. Elbasan, also in the north, became the main industrial town.

But Albania's break with the Soviet Union was painful. Between
1956 and 1960 the Soviet Union had financed 8% of all Albanian
investment and a much higher proportion of industrial investment. Albania's five-year plan was geared to deliveries of machinery and equipment
from the Soviet Union and Eastern Europe. Its domestic industry, agriculture and transport were based on imports from the Soviet Union.
When those ceased abruptly in 1961, the lack of spare parts became an
acute problem, so much so that in 1967 Albania's main engineering
plants were switched to the production of spare parts.

In 1978 there came another abrupt and painful change – the break with
China. This forced Albania to scrap plans for three new ferro-chrome
plants designed to produce chrome for the Chinese market. Chrome
exports were re-directed to other markets, including those in Eastern
Europe and the Soviet Union. Unfortunately for Albania, the ferro-
chrome plant the Chinese had already built, at Elbasan, has 1930s technology that has caused constant production problems as well as large-
scale pollution. A 1990 UN report, commissioned by the Albanian
government, suggested that since most of the industrial plant of this kind
was completely outdated it should be closed down. The truth is that all of
Albania's major industries are stuck with outdated technology that
should be scrapped – it remains a symbol of the disaster inflicted on the

country by the isolationist policies of the Hoxha era.

After Hoxha's death in 1985, Ramiz Alia continued his predecessor's policy of cautiously opening up contacts with a wide range of countries. Albania increased its trade with a number of West European countries, notably West Germany. It also strengthened its trade links with Eastern Europe, particularly Czechoslovakia, East Germany and Romania. Commercial relations with the Soviet Union and the United States, the two 'imperialist' superpowers, remained ruled out on ideological grounds. Trade with Yugoslavia, despite strained relations, continued and expanded, accounting for about 15% of Albania's total trade during the 1980s. Tourism could prove to be a source of hard-currency earnings. Only 30,000 tourists visited Albania in 1990, but the industry could develop, particularly with Western help.

Agriculture still employs about 60% of the labour force, the main crop being maize, sugar beet, wheat and potatoes. It was here that the regime's economic policy suffered its most spectacular defeat: the result of a combination of primitive farming methods, bad planning, inefficient management of labour and resources, and lack of investment. Albania introduced large-scale collectivization only in the 1950s but left most of its mountain agriculture in private hands. In 1967, however, the government embarked on a policy of total collectivization which involved amalgamation of the newly collectivized mountain villages with those in the nearby lowlands. Private plots, which had been responsible for a significant share of the output of milk, eggs and meat, were reduced to a minimum and effectively killed off. Great shortages ensued. Throughout the 1970s Albania had to make up its grain deficit by imports. Poor distribution – lack of refrigeration facilities, transport and so on – was one of the main causes of the deeply unpopular food shortages and most of the waste. By the 1980s these difficulties had become part of a full-scale crisis that engulfed the whole economy.

The main factors in the economic crisis were stagnating agricultural production, failure to reach export targets, decline in the output of oil and chromite, and last but not least population growth on a scale bound to lead to increased social tensions. Albania has a population growth rate of 3%, the highest in Europe. Its population doubled between 1923 and 1960 to over 1.6m and then again to 3.5m by 1980. To relieve the situation, the regime decided in March 1990 to allow private ownership of family livestock, but that led to a reduction in the output of state farms, causing a drastic cut in meat and vegetable supplies to the cities and increasing consumer discontent there.

This economic misery – made more intolerable in the eyes of many Albanians by their ability to watch Italian, Greek and Yugoslav television – was one of the sparks that ignited the revolt in 1990–91 and led to the attempted exodus to Greece, Yugoslavia and across the Adriatic to Italy.

## Romania

Like Albania, Romania based its economic strategy under the communist regime on the hope that its natural resources (particularly oil) would allow it a fast industrial development. But the Soviet Union under Khrushchev had other ideas for Romania: it was to be Comecon's granary. Romania rejected these plans and broke away from Soviet economic control in the early 1960s in order to become an industrial power in its own right and a significant exporter to world markets. Its remarkable effort, starting in the mid-1960s, to reduce its trade dependence on the rest of Comecon, particularly the Soviet Union, met with some initial success: by the early 1970s more than 50% of its trade was with the non-communist world and about 19% of its entire trade was with the European Community. In 1976 Romania became the first Soviet-bloc country to break ranks by opening direct contacts with the European Commission in Brussels. This led in 1980 to the signing of a five-year preferential agreement with the EC. Romania's exports to West Germany, its most important trading partner in the West, exceeded imports in 1970–71, 1977 and 1980–81. Its trade with the United States and Israel also grew significantly.

For all that, the expected large boost to Romania's hard-currency earnings from sales to Western markets failed to materialize. The hope, in Romania as in many other East and Central European states, had been that success in foreign trade would serve to push growth rates sharply upwards. With that expectation Romania had accumulated a hard-currency debt of nearly $10 billion. In 1982 and 1983 it was obliged to ask its Western creditors for debt-rescheduling. Romania's export drive had failed to yield the expected results because, especially in the middle of a world recession, its products – like Bulgaria's – failed to measure up to the competitive conditions on the world market.

Romania's development strategy had proved flawed. This was partly the usual East European obsession with building costly and uneconomic steelworks and other heavy industrial plant. Thus Romania produced in the 1980s about 90% of all the capital goods it required, a policy that helped to widen the technological gap between it and the West still further. Even more important was the concentration on developing the chemical and petrochemical industries. Romania's leaders were aware that the country's oil reserves were becoming depleted, but they had hoped to compensate for this by cheap oil imports from Iran and other oil-producing third-world states, with which Romania had developed a successful trading relationship. The 1973 oil price shock destroyed the basis of this Romanian strategy. Oil prices went up but not those of oil products – at least not sufficiently to make up for the much higher crude oil prices Romania found itself obliged to pay to OPEC countries. Because of its policy of avoiding reliance on the Soviet Union for crucial products, Romania was not participating in the intra-Comecon system of preferential oil prices that the Soviet Union granted to its other partners.

The Romanian regime was well aware of its international financial vulnerability in, for example, the United States Congress, where the extension of most-favoured nation (MFN) status had to be debated annually in the light of Romania's record on such issues as freedom to emigrate. But the policy-related conditions of the International Monetary Fund (IMF) were unacceptable to President Ceausescu, who instead opted in 1984 for a policy of austerity to improve the balance of payments. The Romanian government reduced its debt from $9.9 billion in 1981 to $2.5 billion in 1987 and less than $1 billion in early 1989. In April 1989, Ceausescu announced that Romania had paid off all its foreign debts, though it proved to be an empty boast.

The policy of austerity had a devastating effect on supplies to the domestic market and on Romania's production capacity. Restrictions on imports of machinery, spare parts and raw materials from the West harmed export production. The official reaction to shrinking exports was yet more restrictions on imports. Meanwhile, the workers' harsh living conditions had an adverse effect on their productivity.

In desperation, Romania was forced to turn to the Soviet Union for extra supplies of energy. But these had to paid for in hard currency and 'hard' goods such as foodstuffs and oil-drilling equipment. Humiliatingly, in view of Romania's earlier defiance, agreements were reached with Moscow under which Romanian industry was to be modernized with the aid of Soviet capital, technology and specialists. The agreements particularly referred to Romania's ailing steel industry. The Soviet Union undertook to deliver complete plants producing oil and gas pipe to Romania. In the end, ironically, it was the spontaneous revolt by people without political leaders, hijacked by a group of disaffected communists

and military leaders, and joined by a few dissidents, that led to
Ceausescu's overthrow and execution by firing squad in December 1989.
Romania is still trying to cope with the terrible aftermath of his regime.

## Yugoslavia

In contrast, Yugoslavia, which was freed by the 1948 Tito–Stalin quarrel
from a commercially and technologically counter-productive orientation
towards the Soviet bloc, quickly developed trade links with the West and
later also with the developing countries, its political partners in the non-
aligned grouping. Since 1945 Yugoslavia has benefited from a large
amount of Western (chiefly American) aid. From the point of view of
Western governments, the policy of 'keeping Tito afloat' and thus denying Yugoslavia to the Soviet Union was a relatively cheap way of
improving the defence of Italy and strengthening the Western Alliance's
strategic position in the southern Mediterranean. The first American
'political' loan to Yugoslavia, worth $20m, was provided by the Truman
administration in September 1949. By 1955, at the end of the first period
of large-scale Western aid, Yugoslavia had received $600m worth of
American economic assistance, of which only $55m was in the form of
repayable loans. Military aid provided by the United States during the
same period amounted to just under $600m. By 1960, Western aid and
'soft' credits had reached $2 billion. Later Western aid continued to be
channelled mainly through international organizations, such as the IMF,
the World Bank and the European Community.

Without massive Western support, Yugoslavia would have found it
extremely difficult, perhaps even impossible, to maintain its independence in the early post-1948 period when it found itself under various
forms of pressure – including an economic blockade – from the Soviet
Union and its allies. Moreover – a fact not often remarked upon in
Yugoslavia or abroad – it was precisely Western aid that enabled the
individual Yugoslav republics to pursue, within the framework of
official 'Yugoslav' economic development policies, their own unstated,
parallel policies. The fact that, in addition to Rijeka, Yugoslavia's largest
commercial port in the northern Adriatic, which was in itself quite
sufficient to carry all the country's traffic and trade, two further ports
were built can be understood only in terms of these unstated but very real
'national' strategies. For example, the port of Koper – built on the small
strip of the Adriatic coast just north of Rijeka that the previously land-
locked Slovenia had gained after 1945 – should be seen as an expression

of Slovenia's ambition to have direct access to the sea, rather than the result of an all-Yugoslav commercial calculation.

This special 'national' development strategy, more appropriate to a small sovereign state than a republic of a federation, can be seen even more clearly in the project of a railway linking Belgrade with Bar in Montenegro, on the southern Adriatic coast close to Albania. The project, which also included the building of a modern port at Bar, the third on the Yugoslav coast, was (quite correctly) criticized as commercially dubious, not least because of the high cost of building a railway through extremely difficult mountainous terrain. But it made sense in the context of land-locked Serbia's search, ever since the nineteenth century, for direct access to the sea. To the Serbs, what recommended the Belgrade–Bar project, discussed on and off since 1879, was that the railway avoided non-Serb (i.e., Croat or Muslim) areas and that the port was situated in Montenegro, regarded by all Serbs (and most Montenegrins) as a Serbian land. After much acrimonious debate among the republics, in which non-Serbs, predictably, objected to the Belgrade–Bar project on grounds both of cost and of commercial non-viability, the railway was eventually completed in 1976.[10]

Distinctive, 'small state' strategies have lain behind the building of most of the double capacity – steelworks and refineries as well as other factories and installations – in individual republics ever since 1945. Even in nationally homogeneous countries, there is competition for investment projects, particularly those involving public money. In multinational Yugoslavia, this competition was something quite different, bound up with the separate national agendas that continued to develop. Naturally, all this increased the cost of the Yugoslav economy, but the attraction to proponents of various 'national' projects was that not only others within Yugoslavia but the non-aligned country's rich foreign backers would help to pay for them.

Foreign backing played an important role in the preparation of Yugoslavia's economic reform in 1965. Crucial assistance came from the IMF, which provided Yugoslavia with $80m worth in special drawing rights (SDR). There was also help from the governments of Britain, Italy, France and the United States. With that reform, Yugoslavia officially embarked on the road to market socialism. Imports were liberalized to provide competition for domestic enterprises. The dinar was devalued to stimulate exports. Many prices previously fixed by the state were freed. Measures to tighten credit for Yugoslav enterprises were introduced. The number of those employed in industry fell for the first time since 1952, as did industrial output.

At the same time, the country's tourist industry was expanded. In 1966 Yugoslavia became the first communist-ruled country to allow its citizens to leave for the West. Those who left included many who had lost their jobs as a result of factory closures under the 1965 reform or who would have done so had they stayed. A welcome boost for the country's balance of payments was provided by hard-currency earnings from tourism and remittances sent home by these Yugoslav *Gastarbeiter* ('guestworkers'). In the early 1970s, about one million of them were working in West Germany and other Western countries, accompanied by several hundred thousand family dependants. In 1967 Yugoslavia passed a law that made it the first communist-ruled country to allow joint ventures with Western firms on its territory.

But there was a strong political and economic backlash against the reform. The party's apparat complained of the growing power of the 'technocracy'. Behind this lay resentment of the increased independence exercised by the managers of more successful enterprises, which threatened the control of the local party bosses. Conversely, enterprises under pressure from the credit squeeze and suffering from the competition of cheaper imported goods appealed to the party for support. Growing redundancy and unemployment figures were set by the opponents of reform against the rising number of private businessmen and artisans. Student demonstrations in Belgrade in June 1968 in favour of more full-blooded socialism, under slogans such as 'Work for everyone, bread for everyone' and 'Down with the red bourgeoisie', frightened top leaders.

Tito, never a reformer himself though prepared to accept changes dictated by political necessity, sounded the retreat. Thus June 1968 marked the beginning of the end of an imaginative attempt to bring Yugoslavia over to the free-market system. Competition, which so many in Yugoslavia had found uncomfortable, was soon replaced by deals among corporate interests. 'Market socialism' was replaced by 'consensus economics' (*dogovorna ekonomija*), brain-child of Edvard Kardelj, Tito's chief ideologist. It was codified in the 1974 Yugoslav federal constitution and a special self-management law in 1976.[11]

One of the consequences of the Kardelj system was the fragmentation of industry into thousands of 'self-managing' units, each with its own bureaucracy. This enabled the party to keep closer control over the 'technocrats' and the bankers in what were denounced as the 'centres of alienated power' – alienated from the party, of course. But there was a high economic price to pay; the smaller units were even more preoccupied with distributing rather than creating wealth than the previous larger ones had been.

According to some estimates, nearly two million 'self-managing' bureaucrats, two for each worker, were spawned by the Yugoslav system in the 1970s. To break up the power of the banks, which had become uncomfortably independent of the party under the reform, the banking system was reorganized into hundreds of local banks, each dominated by local political bureaucracies and serving, almost literally, as cash points for individual enterprises. Perhaps most disastrously of all, each of these banks was allowed to raise capital abroad. With plenty of petrodollars available in the aftermath of the 1973 oil crisis, and with Tito acting as Yugoslavia's credit card, the country's banks, however small and obscure, had no difficulty in raising all the capital they wanted.

In some ways, this scramble for foreign loans was inevitable, given the general shortage of capital under the Yugoslav system. Under that system, first applied in industry in the early 1950s and then extended to the entire public sector, 'self-managing' units had little or no interest in setting up subsidiaries in other parts of the country and investing in them because because legally they had no direct control over those offshoots. Each of them, having been set up with the capital of the 'home' enterprise, automatically obtained the status of an autonomous 'self-managing' unit, complete with its own bureaucracy and the right to distribute income as it saw fit. The freedom to borrow abroad at what was, given Yugoslavia's inflation rate, a negative rate of interest proved irresistible. In the mid-1970s, the country went on a borrowing spree which in turn fuelled a huge investment boom. No thought was given to how those debts would be repaid. There was, at the same time, no reason for any of these Yugoslav borrowers to worry because if anything went wrong they could be sure that, in one way or another, the political bosses of their given city, district or republic would arrange their financial rescue. This situation was aptly summed up by Professor Dusan Bilandzic, one of the most acute analysts of the Yugoslav system, in his description of Yugoslavia as 'a country where profits are nationalized and losses socialized'.[12]

Here lay the roots of Yugoslavia's steadily increasing inflation. The state needed to print ever more money to support an inefficient economy, with its hordes of parasitic 'self-managing' bureaucrats and, in addition, to finance a large army and a generous pensions system for Tito's wartime partisan veterans. Perhaps uniquely in the world, the number of these veterans, instead of declining, went on growing from year to year –

owing to the attraction of the privileges attendant on ex-partisan status and the ease with which, in easy-going 'Yugotopia', evidence proving participation on the right side in World War II could be obtained.

By the end of 1980, Yugoslavia's foreign debt stood at just below $18 billion, a large enough figure to cause alarm to Western bankers and governments. In the first half of that year, Yugoslavia's foreign trade deficit was, at $3.5 billion, 8% higher than in the same period the previous year. Worries about Yugoslavia were reinforced by the death in May 1980 of President Tito, who had been the guarantor of its stability for four and a half decades and its best credit card. The so-called 'Long-term Stabilization Programme', launched in July 1983 with the assistance of a large financial aid package prepared by Western governments, had no effect. Yugoslavia's economic and financial slide continued relentlessly. In 1989 its inflation reached an annual rate of 2,500%.

Hopes that Yugoslavia might at last be returning to the path of radical free-marketry first embarked upon in 1965 were raised by the appointment in March 1989 of Ante Markovic – a former prime minister and later president of Croatia and before that a successful industrial manager – as Yugoslavia's prime minister. In December of the same year, the Markovic government pegged the Yugoslav dinar to the Deutschmark (at a rate of 7:1) and made it freely convertible, having previously amassed more than $10 billion worth of hard-currency reserves. Inflation was halted almost immediately. Other fundamental reforms, aimed at turning Yugoslavia into a market economy and including a reform of enterprises (which effectively abolished self-management) and of the banking system (which restored the independence of the banks from local interests) were also launched.

But it became evident in 1990 that there was no political consensus among the republics over the Markovic programme, which remained stalled as a result of strong opposition from various quarters. Croatia and Slovenia broadly supported his policies, but with reservations. Above all, they feared that a strengthening of the federal centre, agreed to on economic grounds, could subsequently, perhaps under a different prime minister, be used to regain central political control as well. Much the strongest opposition came from Serbia, Yugoslavia's largest but also economically most troubled republic. Serbia objected to Markovic's import liberalization policy and his drastic squeeze on credit to loss-making enterprises, seeing both – quite correctly – as a threat to its bankrupt industries.

Even before the outbreak of armed conflict in Slovenia and Croatia in

June 1991, there emerged an important new element in the situation – a certain 'Yugoweariness' in the West, which manifested itself in a reluctance to undertake unconditional financial rescues of Yugoslavia. Some of the old readiness to help a country in which so much Western effort has been invested over the years still survived, but nothing was unconditional any longer. Help had to be justified in each individual instance as against other claims on Western resources. This reflected, more clearly than anything else, Yugoslavia's – but also the whole area's – loss of strategic importance in the post-cold war era. For all four Balkan countries it has been an ominous development.

### A Balkan backwater?

Politically motivated aid in a variety of forms sustained all the four Balkan countries considered here throughout the postwar era. That aid helped make up for the serious deficiencies of communist economic policies. It helped the local regimes to get away without any serious reforms and thus to stay more securely in power and, ultimately, postpone the day of reckoning. That day has now arrived. Tragically, at the very time when really fundamental change is occurring (unlike previous bouts of tinkering with the old system), and when these countries desperately need foreign investment and technical aid to help them with the speedy transition from communism to post-communism, international interest in them has waned.

This is due, not least, to the intense competition for Western goodwill over matters such as debt repayment and trade concessions from countries regarded as 'better bets' to succeed: Czechoslovakia, Hungary, Poland and, of course, the former East Germany. The bleak economic outlook will make the political reshaping of the Balkans, which is already in progress, far more complicated and dangerous. It is a vicious circle, for it will be the area's success in carrying out its own political restructuring relatively peacefully and achieving a degree of political stability reasonably quickly that will determine its chances of attracting foreign investment. And the omens are not good – in either the political or the economic field, for the two are inextricably linked.

All four Balkan states share the main political, economic and social problems involved in the transition from communism to post-communism. But there is one crucial difference between Yugoslavia on the one side and Albania, Bulgaria and Romania on the other. In Yugoslavia, it is not only the remnants of the communist political and economic system that are being dismantled but also the multinational state itself.

Both Bulgaria and Romania will have to cope with the difficult problem of making a go of their economies while at one and the same time trying to satisfy their respective Hungarian and Turkish minorities' demands for human rights and political representation and not allowing the extreme Bulgarian and Romanian nationalists to exploit any backlash among the majority population against such concessions. This will be hard enough, particularly given the serious economic situation both the countries are in, but it is not too rash to predict that, in the foreseeable future – give or take a few territorial adjustments – Bulgaria and Romania will remain sovereign states in more or less the same shape as today.

Albania's transition to democracy will be made more difficult by its extreme poverty and by its lack of a democratic tradition. Its reformers will face opposition from extreme nationalists over the granting of human and political rights to the country's Greek minority, which was subjected for decades to considerable cultural repression by the communist regime. Albania's vulnerability over domestic minority questions will influence its choice of foreign policy partners.

Nevertheless, despite all these problems, no one is actively challenging the existence of Albania as such, nor are the Bulgarian or Romanian states likely to be called into question. But the same is emphatically not true of Yugoslavia. Its fate will affect everyone in the area. Indeed, the future shape of the Balkans largely depends on where the fragments of this now disintegrating state end up: outside, as new entities gravitating, singly or in groups, towards new partners; or perhaps, yet again, within a another Yugoslav framework. The next chapter analyses the deeper reasons for Yugoslavia's crisis and speculates on its possible outcome.

# 5
# TURMOIL IN YUGOSLAVIA

There are many reasons for the crisis in Yugoslavia, but the principal one is that the country's main nations have come to reject it – at least in its present form – as not measuring up to their very different and often mutually exclusive needs and aspirations.

For the Serbs, Yugoslavia's largest nation, the chief trouble has been that there was too little Yugoslavia. And that what there was was far too loose, hardly a 'functioning federation', and therefore (if it was to survive) it needed to be tightened up at the centre. Others, the non-Serb majority, thought that, on the contrary, there was still too much Yugoslavia. They wanted it either broken up into completely independent states or, possibly, turned into a loose grouping ('confederation') of sovereign states, cooperating within a version of the Common Market.

Until recently, such views were of purely academic interest. For three and a half decades after World War II, Yugoslavia was held together by a strong and successful leader at the head of a loyal Communist Party. Moreover, fear of falling under Soviet domination created a bond between outright supporters of Tito's regime and those who opposed it, which also helped to keep the state together. Another cohesive factor was the country's growing prosperity during the last two decades of Tito's life, which created a mood of optimism and hope. Last but by no means least, whatever its citizens thought of Yugoslavia, whether or not they wanted it, the outside world did. In the eyes of the West, Yugoslavia was an important asset during the cold war. To keep it afloat, the West was prepared to reach into its pocket.

Now all of these cohesive factors are gone. Tito died in 1980, the

Map 4 Yugoslavia in 1974

AUSTRIA
HUNGARY
ROMANIA
ITALY
BULGARIA
GREECE
ALBANIA

SLOVENIA
Ljubljana
Koper
Rijeka

C R O A T I A
Zagreb
Knin

BOSNIA &
HERCEGOVINA
Sarajevo
Vrbas

Drina

VOJVODINA
Novi Sad
Belgrade

S E R B I A

SANDZAK

MONTE
NEGRO
Titograd
Bar

KOSOVO
Priština

MACEDONIA
Skopje

A D R I A T I C   S E A

miles
km
20  40  60  80  100
50   100   200

Republican boundary
Provincial boundary

© Vladimir Pavlinic, 1991

country went bust almost immediately afterwards, and the cold war ended in 1989. The Communist Party, for long split into six republican and two provincial parties and also divided along ideological lines into reformist and 'dogmatic' wings, finally broke up at the abortive Congress in Belgrade in early 1990. What happens to Yugoslavia is, for the first time in its history, for its peoples to decide. But they disagree profoundly about what should happen next. Ironically, what most of them do agree about is that most of them think they have had a raw deal in Yugoslavia.

## The Serbs

The most vocal complainants about Yugoslavia for years, particularly since the mid-1960s, have been the Serbs, its largest nation (comprising 36% of the total population, according to the 1981 census,[13] down to 35% according to the provisional results of the March 1991 one). The Serb case against today's federal Yugoslavia was most clearly set out in the draft Memorandum prepared in 1985 by a working group of the Serbian Academy of Sciences in Belgrade under the chairmanship of Antonije Isakovic, its Vice-President and one of Serbia's most prominent writers. This document put forward three main objections to today's Yugoslavia from the Serbian point of view:

(1) The federal government's alleged discriminatory policy towards Serbia in the economic field, and the predominance in economic decision-making ever since 1945 of Croatia and Slovenia, the two western republics. At the root of this, the authors alleged, lay the anti-Serb bias in the pre-1941 Communist Party of Yugoslavia and the Comintern in Moscow.

(2) The partition of Serbia into three parts under Tito's 1974 Constitution: Serbia proper and the autonomous provinces of Vojvodina and Kosovo. These two provinces had existed since the early days of the regime but it was only after 1974 that they were allowed direct participation in decision-making at the federal level, bypassing Serbia.

(3) The allegedly anti-Serb policy pursued in Kosovo by Albanian 'separatists' and 'irredentists' (with support from non-Serb republics), which the authors blamed for the steady exodus of Serbs.

The Memorandum also dealt with the position of the Serbs in Croatia (11.6% of that republic's total population), alleging that they were being discriminated against and subjected to 'genocide'. The authors of the document saw as the guiding principle behind all these policies the slogan 'strong Yugoslavia, weak Serbia' and called for its reversal, especially the abolition of the 1974 Constitution, under which Kosovo and Vojvodina were allowed to evolve into *de facto* republics. The document's main conclusion was that under Tito (who was part Croat and part Slovene) and his Slovene second-in-command, Edvard Kardelj, the Serbs had been treated unfairly in Yugoslavia.[14]

Contrary to what was widely alleged at the time of its publication, the Memorandum did not show that the Serbs were rejecting Yugoslavia as such but only Tito's version of it. Behind this Serbian backlash against Tito's Yugoslavia lay an almost palpable nostalgia for the first, royalist, Yugoslavia. This was echoed in numerous articles and books that followed the Memorandum's publication. The general Serbian view that emerged then was that, despite the pre-1941 kingdom's many imperfections, not least the fact that it was not called Serbia, it was a state the Serbs could identify with and indeed call their own, because at least it assured them a leading role.

The Serbian Academy's Memorandum, rejected by Yugoslavia's non-Serbs as a tendentious, propagandistic compilation, is now generally regarded among the Serbs as a seminal document and the modern equivalent of *Nacertanije* (Outline), the national programme for a Greater Serbia prepared in 1844 by Ilija Garasanin, Serbia's Minister of the Interior. According to Garasanin, that state was to be the successor to the short-lived fourteenth-century Serbian state of King Stefan Dusan, and would take in all Serbs. But Garasanin did not mean only the Serbs (and the Montenegrins, who were Orthodox like the Serbs and traditionally regarded as part of the Serbian nation), but also the Croats, the Bosnian Muslims and the Macedonians.

If the Memorandum provided a theoretical basis for Serbian reassertion in Yugoslavia in the post-Tito period, action was provided by Slobodan Milosevic, who became Serbia's party leader in 1986, a year after the Memorandum's publication. Within a year he was acclaimed as the right man to lead what has since come to be known among the Serbs as *treci srpski ustanak* (the third Serbian uprising), an allusion to the two that occurred in the nineteenth century against the Turks.

Milosevic, a hardline communist but also a brilliant populist politician in tune with the frustrations of the Serbs, found the starting point for his campaign of Serb reassertion among the Serb minority in Kosovo. In 1389 the Turks had inflicted on them in Kosovo Polje a heavy defeat that eventually led to their loss of independence and subjection to Ottoman rule for the next five centuries. Recovery of Kosovo became the Serbs' constant hope and aim. By 1912, however, when Serbia did regain Kosovo from the Turks, the bulk of the Serbs there had left, whereas the number of Albanians had increased.

Principally because of the Albanians' high birth-rate, this demographic trend has accelerated. The 1961 census, for example, listed 646,605 Albanians living in Kosovo (67.2% of the total population). By the time of the 1981 census, their number had increased to 1,226,736 (77.4% of the total). According to the provisional estimates in March 1991 (Kosovo Albanians boycotted the census), their number has gone up to 2 million in the province and 2.4 million in the whole of Yugoslavia. Meanwhile, the number of Serbs had fallen from 227,016 in 1961 (18.4% of the province's total population) to 209,498 in 1981 (13.2% of the total). The same provisional 1991 estimates suggest that the Serb proportion of Kosovo's population has now dropped to well below 10%, while the Albanian one has leapt to above 90%.

A second main factor here has been steady Serbian emigration from the province. The Serbs have blamed this on local Albanian 'terror', which – they claim – has been aimed at driving out all the Serbs and creating an 'ethnically pure' Kosovo. The Albanian response to these Serbian accusations has been that Kosovo's Serbs have actually been glad to be able to get out of the province, which is Yugoslavia's poorest region, with a high unemployment rate and bleak economic prospects. This view is supported by impartial observers.[15] The Albanians also claimed that the Serbs had a strong financial incentive to leave: the land-hungry Albanians, with their large families, were prepared to pay handsomely (often in hard currency earned by Albanian *Gastarbeiter* in the West) for their houses and farms.

Milosevic skilfully exploited the allegations about Albanian 'terror' against the Serbs of Kosovo to build a new and aggressive populist movement. He paid a dramatic visit to the province in the spring of 1987 and met the local Serbs, who complained to him that the ethnic Albanians had maltreated them and that the local (mostly ethnic Albanian) police had failed to give them proper protection. Milosevic promised the Kosovo Serbs that 'nobody would ever beat them again'. In the autumn of 1987 he used their alleged plight to attack the previous leadership in Serbia, including his own mentor, Ivan Stambolic, for having been 'too weak' on Kosovo. Milosevic carried out a thorough purge in the Serbian Communist Party to consolidate his own position.

In response to Milosevic's demands for more 'law and order' in

Kosovo, a federal police unit was dispatched there in October 1987. As a concession to Serbian feelings, Fadil Hoxha, an old partisan who had been Yugoslavia's Vice-President under Tito and who was the most senior ethnic Albanian figure in the party, was expelled. Throughout the summer of 1988 Milosevic's supporters, 'bussed' from Kosovo and other parts of Serbia, staged a series of huge rallies in various parts of the republic. In October 1988, after one such rally in Novi Sad, the capital of the Vojvodina province, a pro-Milosevic group was installed in power there. After several rallies held in Montenegro's capital, Titograd, a pro-Milosevic group came to power there, too, in January 1989.

In Kosovo, meanwhile, unrest continued among the Albanian majority over the increasing police repression. A general strike in February 1989 was followed by a hunger strike by miners in the Trepca lead and zinc mining complex in protest against the impending constitutional changes, which would deprive the province of its autonomy and effectively reintegrate it fully into Serbia. With the backing of the Yugoslav army and the federal security forces, the Serbian police units brought in from Serbia proper and Vojvodina crushed the Albanian protest after unrest throughout the province which lasted six days and claimed 24 lives, all of them ethnic Albanians. In early March 1989, 44 ethnic Albanians, including political and industrial leaders (among them Azem Vllasi, the former party leader) were arrested and charged with inciting rebellion.

On 23 March 1989 Kosovo's Assembly, ringed by Yugoslav army tanks, gave its reluctant assent to the constitutional changes demanded by Belgrade; Vojvodina (fully under the control of pro-Milosevic forces) had already done so. On 28 March Serbia's Assembly adopted the, constitutional amendments, giving the Serbian authorities in Belgrade direct control over Kosovo's police, courts and territorial defence – with an extra amendment thrown in enabling the Serbian Assembly to take decisions affecting Kosovo without first consulting that province's own Assembly.

These events raised Milosevic's popularity to unprecedented heights among the Serbs – not just those in the three parts of Serbia but throughout Yugoslavia. Milosevic's success in presenting himself as the indispensable champion of all Serbs throughout Yugoslavia was an important factor in his electoral victory at Serbia's first multi-party election in December 1990. He was re-elected President of Serbia with a large majority of votes and, under him, the Socialist Party of Serbia (the renamed Communist Party) also won, helped by its tight control of the media, a spot of ballot-rigging here and there and, last but not least, the fact that ethnic Albanians in Kosovo boycotted the election *en masse*, giving Milosevic a number of extra, totally uncontested, seats.

Since then, not least because of Serbia's parlous economic condition, the opposition has made some headway against the ruling party, but on the crucial issue of the national programme for a Greater Serbia there is agreement between the communist regime and the non-communist opposition.

Among non-Serbs, however, the whole Serbian counter-offensive – starting with the Memorandum and reaching its climax with Milosevic-inspired efforts to destabilize Croatia and Bosnia and Hercegovina by inciting local Serbs in these two republics against their democratically elected non-communist governments – has served to strengthen the already strong feelings, particularly in Croatia and Slovenia, against Yugoslavia.

The publication of the Academy's Memorandum in 1985 caused shock and much anger. The document was criticized for its anti-market, *dirigiste* economic assumptions, but above all it caused offence as a manifestation of revived Greater Serbian ambition. The Milosevic offensive which followed confirmed the widespread conviction that the Serbs were bent on restoring their hegemony in Yugoslavia on the pretext of strengthening the country's admittedly weak and ineffectual central government. By then, however, the Slovenes and the Croats had reached the conclusion that they wanted only an absolute minimum of Yugoslavia – if any at all. Milosevic simply strengthened that feeling.

**The Slovenes**
This change in attitude towards Yugoslavia is particularly striking among the Slovenes. Once the most fervent supporters of Yugoslavia, the Slovenes had started having doubts about it in the 1960s. By the mid-1980s, total disenchantment had set in. Various factors, some of them going back a long time, played a role in this volte-face.

One of the earliest reasons for Slovene misgivings was the revival in the early 1960s of the idea of 'integral Yugoslavism' (*Jugoslovenstvo*). This was inspired by the new Yugoslav Communist Party programme adopted at the Party Congress in 1958, and envisaged an eventual merging of separate national cultures into a single Yugoslav culture within the context of a Yugoslav patriotism that would transcend individual loyalties.

This campaign was taken seriously because it was led by people like Dobrica Cosic, a Serbian writer then close to Aleksandar Rankovic, the hardline head of the Yugoslav secret police and former party cadre secretary. Rankovic, who was himself a Serb, seemed at that time likely to succeed Tito. To the Slovenes and Yugoslavia's other non-Serbs, *Jugoslovenstvo* looked suspiciously like a new version of King Alexander's attempt after 1929 to create a hybrid 'Yugoslav nation' – which in reality meant Serbianization.

As a small nation owing its survival principally to the fact that it had managed to keep its culture, notably its national language and literature, Slovenia was not having any of that. With the tacit support of the Slovene Party's Central Committee, the concept of 'Yugoslavism' was attacked in *Borba*, the chief party newspaper, by Dusan Pirjevec, a well-known Slovene Party intellectual. Cosic replied and a long and bitter polemic followed. It ended in a draw because both Cosic and Pirjevec had their highly-placed backers in the party. But the purpose had been achieved. Slovenia had made its point.

Another controversy, which also illustrates Slovene sensitivity over culture, took place in the early 1980s. It was over plans for an all-Yugoslav 'core' educational curriculum in all secondary schools for subjects like history and literature. Thanks largely to strong Slovene opposition, the project – like the earlier *Jugoslovenstvo* one – was dropped amid strong polemics between Serbian and Slovene intellectuals.

Other factors contributed to Slovene disillusionment with Yugoslavia: the heavy burden of high financial contributions to the federal exchequer (including a large federal army and civil service) at a time of economic crisis; the Serbian occupation of Kosovo, the huge costs of which were borne by the whole of Yugoslavia (including Slovenia) but with only Serbia having any say in the handling of Kosovo affairs; the growing Serbian obstruction on the economic front from the mid-1980s onwards, including trade boycotts against Slovenia, special tariffs on Slovene goods and, to crown it all, the monetary 'coup' in December 1990, in which a financially desperate Serbian government, using its own National Bank, 'helped itself' to $1.7 billion worth of money from the Yugoslav National Bank (the bulk of the fresh money supply earmarked for 1991); and, most important, the threat of the imposition of a new, strongly Serbian-flavoured centralist regime under Milosevic that would curtail Slovenia's autonomy.

The really new and important element in the situation was that

Slovenia felt not only that it would like to cut loose from Yugoslavia but that it could actually afford to do so. It no longer saw the old Yugoslav haven as indispensable for national survival. For many years Slovenia has enjoyed excellent bilateral relations with its two prosperous and peaceful neighbours, Austria and Italy. Since 1978 there has also been varied and successful multilateral cooperation within the framework of the *Alpe-Jadran* (Alpen–Adria) regional grouping, an originally Italian idea for a 'working community' that includes, in addition to Croatia and Slovenia, four northern regions of Italy, five Austrian *Länder*, Bavaria and the three western regions of Hungary.

## The Croats

For the Croats, too, the second largest nation after the Serbs, Yugoslavia had at one time seemed a welcome prospect. At the end of World War I, they were glad to get out of their association with Hungary, which had lasted for many centuries, but new dangers loomed from the south. Italy had been promised most of the Croatian Adriatic coast, (including the islands) as an inducement, under the 1915 Treaty of London, to join the war on the Entente's side. At the end of 1918, in the wake of Austria–Hungary's collapse, Italy was thus busy occupying the territories promised to it. For the Croats, union with Serbia, itself an Entente coalition member, within a new Southern Slav state seemed the best protection against these Italian claims.

But post-1918 Yugoslavia proved a bitter disappointment to the Croats. This was not only because it failed to stop Italy from acquiring much of the territory promised under the Treaty of London. A deeper reason was that in Yugoslavia Croatia lost the autonomous status it had enjoyed up to 1918 as one of the 'historic' nations of the Habsburg empire under the *Nagodba* (Compromise) that Croatia signed with Hungary in 1868, a year after the Austro-Hungarian *Ausgleich*. Under an agreement reached in August 1939, on the eve of the outbreak of war, Croatia was made an autonomous unit (*Banovina Hrvatska*), but this gave it less actual autonomy than before 1918. Moreover, the agreement was rejected by the Serbian opposition. This echoed the vehement reaction of Serbian public opinion in 1937 against a proposed concordat with the Vatican, which would have given the Roman Catholic church equality of status with the Serbian Orthodox church: the public demonstrations led by the Serbian Orthodox Patriarch had forced the government to give up the idea.

71

The lack of full recognition of traditional Croat identity and national autonomy in the unitary Yugoslav state aggravated the Croats' sense of insecurity with regard the Serbs. Unlike the Slovenes, who were geographically and linguistically insulated from the rest of Yugoslavia, the Croats felt more threatened by the possibility of Serbianization (disguised as campaigns for 'Yugoslavism'). Before 1941, the ideological basis for this Yugoslav 'unitarism' was the theory that the Croats, the Serbs and the Slovenes (nobody then talked of Macedonians or Bosnian Muslims as separate entities) were three sections or 'tribes' (*plemena*) of one Yugoslav people. In practice, their linguistic closeness – originally supposed to form a solid basis for hopes of a more harmonious common life than, for example, links with non-Slavs like the Germans, the Hungarians or the Italians – turned out to be a factor of division.

It is ironic, in view of their massive wartime participation in the ranks of the victorious partisans, that the Croats should have felt alienated, 'a nation on probation' within their own republic of the Yugoslav federation, forever suspected of not being wholehearted in their attachment to the system and Yugoslavia itself. One explanation for this was that Croatian Serbs, who still had fresh memories of their attempted extermination under Ante Pavelic's Croat wartime state, were predominant in the party, the police, the influential old partisans' association and the key managerial and administrative posts in Croatia. The Serbs comprise only 11.6% of Croatia's population but they made up 19.4% of all party members in 1987 (actually more because a substantial proportion of party members in Croatia describing themselves as 'Yugoslav' – 17.9% – were also Serbs). The proportion of Serbs to Croats remained much higher in the party apparat, the police and the Yugoslav army. Unsurprisingly, therefore, all manifestations of Croat national feeling were immediately branded by the authorities as 'separatism', 'nationalist extremism' and a threat to 'brotherhood and unity'.

This was what happened in 1967 with a 'Language Declaration', signed on behalf of 18 Croat cultural institutions by 140 prominent scholars, writers and other intellectuals (including Miroslav Krleza, Croatia's then greatest living writer, a member of the Croatian Central Committee and a personal friend of Tito's). The Declaration demanded not only constitutional recognition but also full equality for four languages – Croatian, Macedonian, Serbian and Slovene, calling for all the federal laws to be published in these four languages (at the time, only three were recognized officially: Macedonian, Serbo-Croat and Slovene). It also demanded the use of standard Croatian in schools and in the mass media throughout the republic, instead of Serbo-Croatian, which was rejected by most Croats as a political language and a manifestation of official 'Yugoslav unitarism'.

The Declaration caused a bitter public row and many of its signatories were expelled from the party. In a bizarre sequel to this linguistic controversy, an orthographic handbook produced in 1971 by leading Croatian grammarians for use in schools and offices was branded as dangerously 'chauvinist' and 'separatist' by the authorities the following year. They ordered the entire printing of 40,000 copies to be burnt – as if it were an urban guerrilla handbook rather than an orthography text.

This happened at the height of the purge in 1971–2 when President Tito, acting partly in response to demands by senior Croatian Serbs, crushed the 'Croatian Spring', a political and national revival that began after the sacking of Aleksandar Rankovic and other senior secret police officials in 1966. The Croatian purge was part of a larger all-Yugoslav crackdown on 'liberals' and 'technocrats', but was much harsher than anywhere else in Yugoslavia. It had a stultifying effect on national political and cultural life in Croatia – just as the suppression of the 1968 'Prague Spring' had done in Czechoslovakia. The result was a strengthening of pro-independence sentiment in Croatia, which found delayed expression in its first multi-party election in April/May 1990, with the overwhelming victory of the Croatian Democratic Union (*Hrvatska Demokratska Zajednica*), a right-of-centre party led by Dr Franjo Tudjman, a historian and a former Tito general. In June 1991 Croatia proclaimed itself a sovereign state preparatory to secession if agreement over a loose confederation was not reached.

Since the advent of Milosevic, with the spectre of revived Serbian hegemonism allied to a version of populist communism stalking the land, the Croats' rejection of Yugoslavia had become total. But it was tempered by the realization that new and serious problems were being caused by the Croatian Serbs' vehement rejection of a more independent status for Croatia within a Yugoslav confederation, let alone full independence. That rejection was partly based on the fears, particularly of the older Serb generation in Croatia, of what could befall the Serbs under another Croat regime but partly also on the (not unjustified) expectation of loss of privileges, subsidies and other benefits that the communist regime gave Croat Serbs, of whom many were police and army officers, party functionaries, or personnel managers likely to lose much of their privileged status under the new non-communist regime, regardless of whether it was Croat or non-Croat. That explains the total alienation of the Serbs in

Croatia from the start.

The events of August 1990 demonstrated that cutting the umbilical cord linking Croatia to Yugoslavia would not be easy. Militant Serbs in the Knin area north of the Adriatic coast staged an armed rebellion against the non-communist Croat government, elected in May of that year. Having conducted their own referendum on the question of autonomy, the Serbs of 11 predominantly Serb districts proclaimed themselves an autonomous region called *Krajina* (from the name *Vojna Krajina* – Military Region – given by the Habsburgs to army-run districts along the borders of the Turkish empire). The Knin irregulars repeatedly cut rail and road links between Zagreb, Croatia's capital, and the Adriatic coast, causing chaos for tourist traffic passing through. Supported openly by the Milosevic regime in Belgrade (and discreetly by the Yugoslav army units stationed in the area), the *Krajina* Serbs later proclaimed themselves, in March 1991, a part of Serbia.

During the first half of 1991, the Serb challenge spread. Armed Serbs in other areas, too, such as Slavonia in northern Croatia, created no-go Serb-only zones. Each time Croatian police were sent in, the Yugoslav army moved in as well, claiming it was stopping ethnic clashes. Although it is a conscript army drawn from all the nations and national minorities of Yugoslavia, an estimated 70% of its officers are Serbs.

Unlike Slovenia, Croatia did not manage to retain any part of the arms and equipment belonging to its territorial defence forces at the time of the political changeover in May 1990. They were quietly impounded by the Yugoslav army, as were most of the arms of the Croat police reserve, and the army refused to sell any more weapons to Croatia. In the wake of the Serb rebellion in August 1990, Croatia hastily trained, in addition to some extra police, about 20,000 or so gendarmes (*specijalci*), arming them with light weapons, including about 10,000 AK-47 automatic rifles and ammunition, bought abroad (mostly from the discarded stocks of the disbanded Communist Party militia, the 'Factory Guard', in Hungary).

Despite the overwhelmingly pro-independence mood in Croatia, the Tudjman administration hesitated a long time over declaring independence from Yugoslavia, pressing instead for a confederal option. This was principally because of Croatia's vulnerability to the combined Serb–army pressure – in contrast to Slovenia, with its 90.5% Slovene population and thus no sizeable hostile minority to oppose and sabotage independence and, just as important, no common border with Serbia. In the end, Croatia declared its independence a few hours before Slovenia did on 25 June but, unlike Slovenia, did not try to take over the border control posts, the action that brought the army down on Slovenia. This did not save it from a concerted attack from a number of directions by Serb irregulars, trained, armed and openly supported by the Yugoslav army. In the early summer of 1991 this 'dirty war' resulted in several hundred (almost entirely Croat) deaths.

## Other nationalities

Standing aside from the main protagonists in the Yugoslav drama now unfolding are the country's other nations and minorities. Unlike in pre-war Yugoslavia, the 'national problem' is no longer a mainly Croat–Serb affair. Tito's federal system gave political recognition to the national identity of the Muslims of Bosnia and Hercegovina, the Macedonians and the Montenegrins, as well as the two biggest national minorities, the Albanians of Kosovo and the Hungarians of Vojvodina. These minorities all matter now, and are playing an important role in the outcome of the current crisis. This has been true both of Bosnia and of Macedonia, with their compromise plans for a peaceful outcome, a sort of civilized parting.

### The Muslims

The two million Muslims (two and a half according to preliminary estimates of the March 1991 census), the largest ethnic component of Bosnia and Hercegovina, are against a centralized Yugoslavia under Serbian domination. Their leadership, elected at the multi-party elections in November 1990, in which the Party of Democratic Action captured virtually the entire Muslim vote, has expressed itself in favour of a loose confederation of sovereign states like that advocated by Croatia and Slovenia. But this has angered the more militant Serbs in Bosnia and Hercegovina and the Milosevic regime in Belgrade.

In April 1991 a number of districts in western Bosnia, where the Serbs have a majority, decided to form an autonomous region within Bosnia and Hercegovina, analogous to the Serbian *Krajina* in Croatia. Some districts in south-eastern Hercegovina announced their intention of joining Montenegro. The Muslims saw these incidents as part of the preparations for the creation of a Greater Serbia that would take in Bosnia and Hercegovina. Their fear was that this would encourage the Croats in western Hercegovina to start demanding inclusion in Croatia.

To the Muslims, division of their republic would be the ultimate nightmare in which they would be the chief losers – although both the

Serbs and the Croats (particularly the Serbs) would also face problems because of the complex and geographically scattered national concentrations within Bosnia and Hercegovina. According to the latest complete census figures available (from 1981), the Muslims make up 39.5% of the republic's population, followed by the Serbs (32%) and then the Croats (18.4%). In 1981, there were 23 districts in the republic with no absolute majority for any of the three national groups; 32 with an absolute Muslim majority; 31 with an absolute Serbian majority; and 14 with an absolute Croat majority.

The national balance is likely to have shifted in the past decade towards a greater Muslim majority, largely because of their higher-than-average birth-rate. (The Muslim percentage has gone up to 42–43%, according to the 1991 census estimates.) It is also likely that some of the 7.9% of Bosnia's inhabitants who declared themselves as 'Yugoslavs' in 1981 will have declared themselves as Muslims in the 1991 census. Even so, the Muslims are unlikely to have achieved an absolute majority, which would enable them to claim the republic as their national state, leaving the Serbs and Croats as minorities rather than, as up to now, equal constituent nations.

Moreover, the untidy geographic distribution of these national groups remains a complicating factor. For example, the bulk of Bosnia's Serbs do not live in areas contiguous to Serbia but in the west and the north-west of the republic close to Croatia, separated from Serbia by large mainly Muslim areas in central and eastern Bosnia. This is particularly true of regions closest to the Drina river, the border between Bosnia and Serbia. There is a strong concentration of Bosnian Muslims on the other side of the Drina, in what used to be the Novi Pazar Sandzak region under the Turks and then became part of Bosnia from 1878 to 1918, only to be divided in 1945 between Serbia and Montenegro. The strongest political party in the former Sandzak area now belonging to Serbia is the same party that represents the majority of Muslims in Bosnia – the Party of Democratic Action.

The Croats represent less of a complication because the bulk of them are in western Hercegovina and north-eastern Bosnia. Both these areas adjoin Croatia and so, in principle at least, it would be easier to hive them off if the whole republic were to be divided. There is a precedent for such a division in the 1939 Croat–Serb agreement, which led to the setting up of an autonomous Croatia ruled by the *ban* (viceroy). The area comprised today's Croatian republic, eastern Srijem (today Serbia), the Boka Kotorska district (today Montenegro), as well as the predominantly

Croat regions of north-eastern Bosnia and western Hercegovina. It had been expected at the time that, under a further reorganization of Yugoslavia, the rest of Bosnia would go to Serbia, but the war intervened.

Bosnia's exposed position between Croatia and Serbia would make it the natural linchpin of any possible future grouping that might replace today's Yugoslavia. Indeed, Bosnia has been in such a situation before. Before 1878, it consisted of historic Bosnian lands between the Vrbas and Drina rivers and of 'Turkish Croatia' – Croat lands occupied by the Turks after 1463 and attached to the Ottoman Bosnian *pashalik* (province). After its removal from the Ottoman empire Bosnia was administered by Austria–Hungary but enjoyed a separate position detached from both halves of the monarchy. This continued even after 1908, when Bosnia was formally annexed by Austria–Hungary.

## The Macedonians

Like the Muslims, the Macedonians on the face of it have a lot to lose from Yugoslavia's break-up. Like the Bosnians, they see the idea of a greater Serbia as a direct threat. It reminds them of Macedonia's old pre-1941 status as 'Southern Serbia', when they were forced to declare themselves as Serbs. Ideally, the Macedonians would prefer Yugoslavia to evolve into a loose confederation of sovereign states, as advocated by Bosnia, Croatia and Slovenia. There is agreement among the Macedonian political parties about that.

But, like the Serbs, they fear that a new Albanian entity might eventually be created within Yugoslavia. This would not be confined to the province of Kosovo but would also take in certain districts of Montenegro, where the Albanians have the majority, as well as the largely Albanian-inhabited western Macedonia, right up to Skopje, the republic's capital. The strongest Macedonian party to emerge from the November 1990 election has come out in favour of full independence and ultimately membership of the European Community. Other Macedonian politicians see this, not entirely incorrectly, as an unrealistic ambition. Meanwhile, there has been some revival of pro-Bulgarian sentiment – though this is nowhere near as strong as before 1914. For the time being, the Macedonians remain a second-division player in the Yugoslav drama. They have much interest in its outcome, but little direct influence.

## The Montenegrins

The same is true of the half-million or so Montenegrins, Yugoslavia's smallest nation, which can boast of a long and colourful history as a

detached but nevertheless integral part – or 'tribe', as it used to be called
– of the wider Serbian nation. In 1918 a referendum decided in favour of
union with the new unitary Yugoslav kingdom. Those Montenegrins
opposed to union were known as *zelenasi* (the Greens), while its supporters were called *bjelasi* (the Whites) – their names deriving from the
coloured ballot-slips used in the referendum. The Greens never gave up
and some of them plumped in 1941 for the Italian offer of an autonomous
Montenegro under an Italian protectorate. After Italy's defeat and surren-
der in 1943, they faded from the scene, totally eclipsed by the overwhelming Montenegrin participation on the communist side in Yugoslavia's civil war. But the establishment of a separate federal republic of
Montenegro under the communists in 1945 represented a victory for the
ideals of the Greens, who take the view that, for all their close connections with the Serbs, the Montenegrins are a separate people.

The Greens' long period of dominance in Montenegro's cultural and
political life ended with the revolt in January 1989 that brought to power
the pro-Milosevic group, an updated version of the old White 'unitarists',
which campaigned on the basis of Milosevic's description of Serbia and
Montenegro as 'two eyes in one head'. These neo-Whites were helped in
their bid for power in the financially bankrupt Montenegro by hopes of
rescue by their Serbian brothers in Belgrade.

As in Serbia, the communists emerged as the strongest party in the
November 1990 election. But hopes of injections of aid from Belgrade
have always been unrealistic and, unsurprisingly, have remained unful-
filled: Serbia itself is in a parlous economic state. This situation has
brought the Greens back into the public debate. For the time being,
however, the pro-Serbian Whites are holding firmly to power, and
Montenegro continues to stand alongside Serbia. The question is whether
these two could impose unity on Yugoslavia, with the support of the
Yugoslav army, the country's 'seventh republic'. The military leaders
showed their commitment to a united communist Yugoslavia by launch-
ing a new Communist Party in November 1990 to fight for just such an
aim. They have repeatedly stated that they would not tolerate the break-
up of Yugoslavia.

**The military option**
The possibility of an army-backed coup to overthrow the present non-
communist governments in Croatia and Slovenia and recreate a centralist
state that would be federal in name only continues to be discussed – and

feared – in Yugoslavia, particularly after the Yugoslav army's humilia-
tion at the hands of the Slovenes in July 1991. It might still happen but
probably won't. This is not because of any reluctance among some
Yugoslav generals – and party hardliners allied with them – to 'have a
go' but, rather, because of their realization that to use Yugoslavia's
conscript army in such a way would risk its collapse. Although most of
its officers and NCOs are Serbs, its recruits are not. For example,
according to official figures, nearly 20% of all recruits are ethnic Albanians. Then there is a high proportion of Bosnian Muslims, not to speak of
Croats and Slovenes. Given all those limitations – especially the difficulty of creating enough 'ethnically reliable' units (in other words,
composed of Serbs and Montenegrins), the army probably could not
hope to gain control over the whole of Yugoslavia.

But even if a coup were carried out, on the pretext of preventing ethnic
clashes in Croatia, and did succeed, any regime produced by it would be
highly unstable and short-lived. One of the factors that would bring it
down would be lack of finance. A Yugoslavia ruled by the military
would be unable to raise foreign credits. It would not be like the authoritarian regimes in countries such as Chile, which provided a stable framework for the transition to a free-market system. A more apt parallel
would be General Jaruzelski's post-1981 military regime in Poland –
except that the Yugoslav version would probably not last as long as
Jaruzelski's. Yugoslavia's strongly communist, anti-Western generals
and admirals do not have the credentials needed to convince Western
bankers and governments of their sincerity and fitness as agents of the
free market. And whereas in the past the Soviet Union might have been
there, ready to give support, now there is nobody else to help with a
military option.

### An irretrievable breakdown?
If uniting Yugoslavia by force is not a serious option, is there really
nothing else that could keep it together? With Tito gone, the Communist
Party no longer in charge and its freed peoples busy quarrelling among
themselves, has Yugoslavia now broken down irretrievably? There is
overwhelming evidence – some of it quoted above – to suggest that this
is indeed so. The conclusion that Yugoslavia has disintegrated totally is
confirmed by the Croat and Slovene independence declarations. But
before we write Yugoslavia off, caution is in order. Could it be that all
these obituaries are premature? After all, Yugoslavia was broken up once

before – fifty years ago, in April 1941 – only to be resurrected by Tito four years later. Besides, historical experience teaches that it usually takes a lost war, with enemy occupation thrown in, or some extraordinary natural calamity for a state completely to break up. But this is peacetime. The inviolability of European frontiers is guaranteed by the 1975 Helsinki Final Act. Far from working for Yugoslavia's break-up, governments and various international institutions are still searching for ways of helping it to survive in some form Could it survive – and evolve, for example, into a confederation comprising several parts, each with autonomous sub-units?

On the face of it, the idea – floated many times in the past – remains just possible but, after the war in Slovenia, it is unlikely. For the deeply disunited peoples of Yugoslavia to sink their differences and come together again, there would have to be some overriding new reason. Even the setting up of a loose confederation is a serious and complicated business, requiring a sense of common purpose and a common aim. Such an aim could be, for example, to avert external danger from a clearly perceived common enemy. The clearly perceived need to defend themselves against a possible Soviet invasion was what brought together France and Germany only a few years after they had fought as bitter enemies in World War II.

That sense of external danger from a Soviet attack and occupation was one of the factors that helped keep Yugoslavia together for such a long time after the break with Stalin in 1948. But now there is no such external enemy to unite against anywhere on the horizon. It is the enemy within – whoever it might be – that the peoples of Yugoslavia fear and want to defend themselves against.

What of other possible reasons for coming together in a common Yugoslav framework – for example, fear of damage to the economies of the individual republics from the fragmentation of the Yugoslav market within which they had all been operating, except between 1941 and 1945, ever since 1918? A few years ago, fear of economic fragmentation and the resulting loss of both markets and sources of raw materials would have been a major deterrent to secessionism. But this potential deterrent has lost most of its force as a result of the dramatic deterioration of economic relations among Yugoslavia's republics since 1988, notably Serbia on the one side and Croatia and Slovenia on the other. In most cases, these economic hostilities have been initiated by Serbia to put political and economic pressure on the other two, but they in turn have not been slow to fight back.

In this inter-republican economic warfare, Serbia's chosen instruments have been boycotts of Croat and Slovene goods, a special duty imposed on the import of such goods, and confiscation of Croat and Slovene companies' branches in Serbia at 'spontaneous' workers' meetings. Retaliation by the two republics has included suspension of payments to central funds for the development of Kosovo until Serbian repression there has stopped; threats to impose special taxes on Serbian weekend cottages in Croatia; refusal by Croatian airports to handle JAT, the Yugoslav state airline (viewed in non-Serb parts of Yugoslavia as a 'Serbian' company) because of non-payment of dues; and duty-free imports of Western cars by Croatia and Slovenia in defiance of current rules designed to protect Yugoslavia's car production, which is centred in Serbia. Croatia's tourism had already been pretty much shattered by the Serb rebellion in some of its most prized tourist areas such as the Plitvice National Park and the Adriatic hinterland. Slovenia's was killed off by the war in June/July 1991, which also destroyed Croatian tourism completely.

This economic breakdown of Yugoslavia has persuaded non-Serbian republics of the need to have their own national currencies. Slovenia has been the first in the field, and has been discussing the possibility of aligning its currency to a European one – most probably the Austrian schilling. Croatia has been making similar plans. In April 1990 Macedonia's leading nationalist party suggested the introduction of a Macedonian currency unit called the *stater*.

Serbia and the army seem to have realized that, even acting together, they cannot force solutions on the whole of Yugoslavia without risking a humiliating loss. Serbia would face enormous difficulties if it tried to impose the 'Greater Serbia' concept advocated by Garasanin and the 1985 Memorandum. Such a state would involve ruling over too many Croats, Bosnian Muslims, Albanians and others to make it governable. Even if it could be set up, it could only survive as a dictatorship. However, there is no evidence to date to suggest that the idea has been abandoned. On the contrary, since the Yugoslav army's defeat in Slovenia there is growing evidence that the Greater Serbia option is being tried.

An eventual compromise could until recently have been based on Serbia's recognition of the present republican borders, in return for agreement by Croatia and Slovenia that some of the powers they had insisted on retaining for themselves could be transferred to future joint institutions. But this looks more and more unlikely. Any agreements made now would necessarily be provisional. Most non-Serbs would regard them as having been reached under duress, with the pro-Serbian army threatening in the background. For many Serbs, any deals reached now would be the best that could be achieved with Milosevic – a domestic and foreign liability – still in power.

Given its history so far, Yugoslavia will most likely continue to dissolve. But the dismantling of this remnant of the Versailles order may still take a while to complete. This slow-motion disintegration will be welcome to some but will, at the same time, pose new challenges not only to the inhabitants of Yugoslavia but also to their neighbours in the Balkans and others beyond.

# 6

# A NEW BALKANSCAPE?

On the face of it, the dismantling of the external spheres of influence controlling the Balkans* should be good news for the peoples of the region, not least for those in and around Yugoslavia likely to be affected in one way or another by the resumption of the 'unfinished business' left over from Versailles. The bad news for everybody in the Balkans – whether they are in favour of change or against it – is that their new internal freedom of manoeuvre has also brought with it the danger of the region's international marginalization. Powerful outsiders may have been calling the tune in the Balkans all these years, but they were at least also paying their Balkan pipers. With the sharp drop of interest in Balkan music, the ex-communist locals face the daunting prospect of having to confront, on their own, the horrendous task of coping with the aftermath of communism and of rebuilding their societies and economies. Can they do it?

The answer is that, like the rest of the former communist-ruled Eastern Europe, they cannot. The political and economic prospects for the ex-communist countries of the Balkans, though perhaps not as bleak as those facing the Soviet Union, are certainly bleaker than those for ex-communist Central Europe. Communism has taken deeper roots there and destroyed more of the previous social and economic structures, which had been far weaker in the Balkans anyway. The transition to political pluralism and the free market has begun, but in some countries

---

*Of course, some external influence remains - in Greece, a member of both the EC and Nato, and in Turkey, which, as well as being a Nato member, has become a close ally of the United States, particularly since the Gulf War in 1991.

(Albania, Bulgaria, Montenegro, Romania and Serbia) the Communist Party under a new (usually Socialist) name, won at multi-party elections in 1990–91. Albania, Bulgaria, Macedonia and Romania now have what, in effect, are coalition governments of communists and non-communists. Yugoslavia, Bosnia and Hercegovina, Croatia and Slovenia have non-communist governments; but even there the old communist cadres remain influential, particularly in the economy. Yugoslavia, which is in many ways more ready than the other Balkan states for the transition to the free-market system, has already had a comprehensive programme for implementing that transition since 1989. It was devised in consultation with Western financial institutions and governments by the federal Prime Minister, Ante Markovic, but the whole programme has been completely stalled for some time now. This is because of the very real conflict of political and economic interests between the more pluralist, Western-oriented and pro-market Croatia and Slovenia on one side and the authoritarian, anti-Western and anti-market Serbia on the other.

Whenever real reform does get under way – as it eventually must – it will place additional strains on the new and still evolving political system. As the example of Poland has shown, those strains will open the way for political manipulation, by populist demagogues, of the inevitable public disillusionment with the various painful phenomena accompanying the reform process – notably mass unemployment. One such politician was the notorious Stanislaw Tyminski, whose X Party won a large number of (chiefly protest) votes at the 1991 presidential election. The prolonged political instability, not only in the rapidly disintegrating Yugoslavia but also (though in a less drastic way) in Albania, Bulgaria and Romania, is meanwhile acting as a deterrent to foreign investment. Such investment is desperately needed to provide a solid basis for long-term growth but also, in the short term, to kindle just enough hope to enable the new political leaders to maintain social tranquillity and political tolerance during the early (and most dangerous) phases of the transition process.

Quite clearly, then, the four formerly communist-ruled states of the Balkans cannot achieve their political and economic salvation alone and unaided. But who is willing to lend a helping hand – and purse? What will, for example, be the attitude of their former imperial overlord and still formidable eastern neighbour, the Soviet Union?

## The Soviet angle

The Balkans may no longer have, for the Soviet Union, their earlier, and even recent, strategic and symbolic importance. But, preoccupied though it is with its own multiple domestic crises, the Soviet Union has by no means abandoned its interest in the Balkans and is showing it in a variety of ways. For example, it was ready after a relatively short interruption in 1990, to resume – and on relatively favourable barter terms, too – oil deliveries to Bulgaria, which was strapped for cash and therefore unable to turn elsewhere in search of alternative sources for the energy it had always received from the Soviet Union. (In 1989 alone, as much as 90% of Bulgaria's crude oil imports came from the Soviet Union.)

There are economic reasons why Moscow should want to continue to trade (for example, it needs food from Bulgaria), but there is also a political calculation: Bulgaria needs to be stopped from straying uncomfortably far into the Western orbit by associating too closely with the three strongly pro-Western Central European countries, Czechoslovakia, Hungary and Poland. Bulgaria has been trying to join the trilateral cooperation scheme launched in February 1991 by these three countries and has even shown keen interest in establishing direct relations with Nato, whose Secretary-General, Manfred Wörner, visited Bulgaria in June 1991. Before that, in March, 135 non-communist members of the Bulgarian National Assembly had signed a proposal that Bulgaria should take the necessary steps to join. All this does not amount to much because Nato has set its face against extending its security cover, directly or indirectly, outside its officially designated area in Europe. But Moscow has traditionally regarded the very idea of one of its neighbouring countries being linked to Nato as totally unacceptable. Hence some concern over Bulgaria, even though, of course, it has no common border with the Soviet Union.

Another sign of Moscow's continuing interest in its former dependencies was the persistence with which it had been pressing for the resumption of diplomatic relations with Albania, a country even farther removed from its borders, and the alacrity with which it accepted Albania's offer to resume them in July 1990. Relations with Albania had been frozen since the famous Khrushchev–Hoxha quarrel in 1961. In May 1991 the Soviet Union sent a large official delegation to Albania to discuss the deepening of political and commercial relations between the two countries. Albania's rapidly worsening economic situation may make the idea of resuming the Soviet economic connection in some form attractive to the present leadership.

For rather more obvious geopolitical reasons – not least the need to keep under control nationalist agitation in the Soviet republic of Moldavia/Moldova (formerly Bessarabia) – the Soviet Union continues to cultivate Romania diligently. In April 1991, Romania surprised the rest of Eastern Europe by the speed with which it agreed to the signing of a new Treaty of Cooperation, Good-neighbourliness and Friendship with the Soviet Union, the first East European country to do so since the dramatic changes in 1989. The treaty, which top Soviet leaders have portrayed as a model for similar new ones with the other East and Central European countries, effectively gives the Kremlin a veto over Romania's foreign policy by stipulating that neither party to the agreement may join an alliance hostile to the other. The three Central European countries have resolutely refused to contemplate signing such an agreement – at least in its Romanian form – and have criticized Romania for doing so.

On the Romanian side, there is clear political and economic calculation behind the move: the Soviet Union is a major source of raw materials as well as an important market for Romania, and it is, besides, a politically significant guarantor of the territorial status quo in Transylvania. In that sense, the treaty is to be seen as a counterweight to Hungary's close and steadily growing links with the West, which Romania of course also wants to join. Romania is jealous of Hungary for having stolen a march on it here. As for Moldavia/Moldova, the regime in Bucharest is playing the issue very carefully, not giving overt encouragement to more radical advocates there of union with Romania. The Romanian–Soviet treaty underwrites the inviolability of all state borders but also makes provision for closer relations between Moldavia/Moldova and Romania proper.

The Soviet Union maintains a close interest in Yugoslavia. It was one of the first foreign countries to be visited, in April 1991, by Alexander Bessmertnykh, shortly after he replaced Eduard Shevardnadze as Soviet Foreign Minister. With an eye on its own nationality problem, the Kremlin – not surprisingly – favours the forces there (particularly the Yugoslav army) that are trying to keep the country together. In July, after a meeting with Chancellor Kohl in Kiev, Mikhail Gorbachev used the outbreak of armed conflict between Slovenia and the Yugoslav federal army as a lesson and a warning to Europe and the Soviet Union that 'what has been built up over many decades by common effort cannot be easily divided' and that 'disintegration cannot be good – it carries with it a huge risk'.[16] Yuli Kvitzinski, a special Gorbachev emissary, visited various Yugoslav capitals in the same month. There have been persistent rumours in Yugoslavia of Soviet and Yugoslav generals plotting together, but these were denied in May 1991 by Soviet embassy officials in Belgrade.

Thus, although the Soviet Union's current influence in the Balkans has been sharply reduced, there is a solid basis from which it can restore close relations if, for example, things should turn sour between the West and the post-communist Balkan states, forcing the latter to turn eastwards. In its present enfeebled state, the Soviet Union could not overnight fill the gap the West refuses to fill any longer. But at some stage in the not-too-distant future, particularly if the West fails to meet exaggerated Balkan expectations of assistance, a revitalized Soviet Union – or Russia – could pick up the threads with one or all of its former Balkan allies. Economic collapse in one or more of these countries could, if the Soviet Union is ready and willing to act, provide it with a 'window of opportunity' to rebuild its influence.

## The Western stake

Whether or not the Soviet Union will, once again, engage itself more actively in the Balkans will depend – quite literally – on the shape it is in and, of course, on the state of its relations with the West. Its continuing close economic dependence on the West seems to rule out, for the moment at least, the resumption of a cold-war-style East/West contest in the Balkans. But even if the Soviet Union became more assertive, as Mikhail Gorbachev seems to be hinting, would this matter in the Balkans, serious though it would be for Central Europe? Should the West care about the Balkans? What, if any, are the real Western interests in the region?

All Western countries, particularly those in Western Europe, would of course like to see a prosperous, reformed Balkan region as a trading partner – not least at a time of recession. That goes without saying. But for the present, given the area's political instability and massive trade and balance-of-payments deficits, economic interest in the Balkans, particularly by private business, remains limited. As far as security aspects are concerned, some Western strategic interests are at stake there now – notably in Greece and Turkey, as already mentioned. As far as the Soviet Union is concerned, in the foreseeable future nobody in the West expects Soviet tanks, for example, to roll into Romania and then on into Bulgaria and Yugoslavia. Any such move would be seen as puzzling (why should Moscow do it?) rather than immediately threatening to the West – though certain conclusions would be drawn from it.

Bismarck once said that the Balkans 'were not worth the bones of a single Pomeranian grenadier'. Is this perhaps the time for the West to revert to Bismarckian scepticism and opt for a policy of 'benign neglect' of the region for the rest of this century and beyond? A tempting thought for Western policy-makers, but also one that has to be resisted. The four impoverished Balkan countries emerging from four and a half decades of communism may have lost most of their former strategic and economic importance. However, there are several (mostly negative) reasons why they cannot be ignored by their neighbours or by other more distant states.

There is also a broader positive thought that binds all the specific reasons for continuing to care about the Balkans into one single argument. It is that, for better or worse, in a Europe which has just seen the end of its post-1945 political division, the cordoning off or 'ghettoization' of any of its parts is no longer possible and therefore should not even be attempted. As the swift Western, especially EC, reaction to the war between Slovenia and the federal army in Yugoslavia at the end of June 1991 and the continuing bloodshed in Croatia showed, it is impossible for the rest of Europe simply to close its eyes to a violent conflict there. The same would be true of Albania if civil war broke out there.

## Moving masses

One of the most obvious ways in which countries pass their troubles on to their neighbours is by sending their refugees to them. Eastern Europe has lately figured in public debates in the West as one of the principal problem areas. While it is true that there may have been some tendency to overdramatize the scale of the possible refugee influx caused by the unsettled political and economic conditions in Eastern and Central Europe, including the Balkans, few would deny that a potentially troublesome problem lurks there.

If, for example, the present truce in Yugoslavia between Slovenia and the army were to break down and merge with a full-scale war between Croatia and Serbia, not a few Yugoslav citizens would seek to escape across the border into one of the neighbouring countries or beyond. It is also on the cards that, if there were a really bloody conflict following an uprising by ethnic Albanians in the Kosovo province, some ethnic Albanians from there might try to escape to Albania. Similarly, some of Yugoslavia's Macedonians may seek refuge in neighbouring Bulgaria in the event of civil strife in their own republic. For the moment, Romania is likely to remain the least favoured destination for would-be refugees from a Yugoslavia torn by political strife and war, but in the event of a crackdown or civil war in the Soviet Union it could expect large numbers from Moldavia/Moldova.

Yugoslavia's other neighbours, too, have very real fears about potentially large numbers of refugees in the near future.

*Austria*, Europe's busiest refugee haven for decades, fearing that it might find itself overwhelmed by a huge new wave from Eastern Europe, has recently reinforced security at its borders with both Hungary and Yugoslavia: the former to stop illegal immigrants from Romania; the latter in response to the war in Slovenia at the end of June 1991.

*Hungary* has had to cope for a number of years with the refugee influx from Romania – both ethnic Hungarians from Transylvania and ethnic Romanians. Its worry is a possible refugee wave from northern Croatia and from Vojvodina all fleeing into southern Hungary from civil war in Yugoslavia.

*Italy*, which has recently been surprised by the arrival of hundreds of Albania's 'boat people' across the narrow Straits of Ottranto, fears much larger contingents coming over from Yugoslavia's Eastern Adriatic shore or by land through Istria if the present conflict becomes prolonged; it has increased its military strength at the Yugoslav border.

*Greece* has for some time now been a place of refuge for those escaping from Albania – members of the Greek minority who have been welcome but also a small number of ethnic Albanians who have not. What Greece fears now is large numbers of people of all nationalities escaping from the south of Yugoslavia if a civil war should spread.

The Balkans' potential for creating refugee problems for other countries does not stop there. *Turkey*, thrust by geography into the forefront of the international relief effort in Iraq, continues to keep a close eye on the situation in Bulgaria for fear of a possible influx of Muslim refugees from there. In 1989, at the height of the conflict between the (then still) communist government in Bulgaria and the country's Muslim community, most of whom regard themselves as Turks, no fewer than 350,000 Muslims left for Turkey. The bulk of those refugees have since returned to a not particularly warm welcome in Bulgaria. The present government – a coalition made up of communists (now renamed Socialists) and non-communists – is striving to ensure greater public tolerance for the Muslims, but some of them might decide to leave again if the situation in Bulgaria deteriorated – whether economically or in terms of human rights. Turkey's current efforts at improving relations with Bulgaria and engaging it into frameworks of cooperation reflect its anxiety over this issue.

Nor would other, more distant, European countries remain unaffected by such Balkan convulsions. Germany would feel the impact if relatives and friends of its own Yugoslav *Gastarbeiter* arrived in large numbers to seek asylum from a disintegrating country amid a civil war. Hostility between national groups – between Croats and Serbs or Albanians and Serbs – could be reflected amongst different *Gastarbeiter* communities. The same could happen in other West European countries with Yugoslav population concentrations, like France, Sweden and Switzerland. Poverty is making many Albanians think of leaving but at the same time stopping them from doing so: most cannot afford the air fare, let alone the hard currency needed to finance even a short stay in the West – though they can, and have been trying to, escape illegally by boat to Italy and across the land border to Greece. Western countries have not been particularly generous with visas. But there could be another wave of would-be refugees across all of Albania's borders as well as the Adriatic if the present situation were to deteriorate still further into chaos.

**A challenge for Europe**
However, refugees are only one – particularly direct and visible – way in which the Balkans could impact on their neighbours and the rest of Europe. There are others, equally visible and no less important. For example, war in Yugoslavia has already disrupted land and air communications and, therefore, also trade and tourist traffic between Western Europe and Greece and Turkey. In a less obvious way, a protracted economic crisis in the Balkans could gradually seep through into neighbouring countries, first affecting trade, tourism and other activities in their frontier regions and then spreading more widely. The likely adverse effects of such a situation should not be overdramatized but they could, nevertheless, be considerable.

The rest of Europe, particularly Western Europe, could probably continue to get by without paying too much regard to the Balkans. Central Europe could not do so, especially as it has already lost so much of its trade with the Soviet Union and the former East Germany: now even the impoverished Balkans still figure as significant trading partners. In fact, what adversely affects Central Europe also has an impact on Western Europe – not only economically but also politically. The whole of the West wants the new pluralist, free-market project in the former communist-ruled Europe to succeed. In an increasingly interdependent Europe, that should mean doing something for the Balkans too. But will it be done and, if so, what?

With the exception of Yugoslavia (which, as we have seen, has long been a special case), the Balkan countries have always been regarded by the West as a lower priority than Central Europe. The often and openly proclaimed guideline for Western policy on economic aid to Europe's former communist-ruled countries has been for some time that it should be concentrated on the three Central European 'hopefuls': Czechoslovakia, Hungary and Poland. This is partly because of their direct strategic, political and economic importance to the West but partly also because these three are, in comparison with the Balkan states, further advanced on the road to the free market and, therefore, better prepared to receive such aid and make good use of it. The scope for other forms of aid to the Balkans, including political and military aid, should in principle be greater, but in practice a similar discrimination operates here too. But that something should be done, within these limitations, for the Balkan states is not in dispute: the question becomes one not of 'if' but of 'who' and 'how'.

*Security*

As far as the security aspect is concerned, there are not many dilemmas. It is already clear that Nato will not be extending a security guarantee to any part of the former communist-ruled part of Europe, not even to the Central Europeans. Preliminary internal discussion has barely begun about a possible role for the Western European Union (WEU), but the scope for action under its auspices will not be clear until its relationship to Nato has been defined. The Conference on Security and Cooperation in Europe (CSCE), which has set up a conflict-resolution centre in its new secretariat in Prague, will eventually have a role to play in watching over the human rights situation in individual countries, perhaps also in offering help and mediation in conflicts over minority issues. It could also stimulate confidence-building measures between individual countries, like the 1990 military cooperation and Open Skies agreements between Hungary and Romania. But as its work is only just starting results should not be expected too soon. At the end of June 1991, at Austria's request, it discussed the situation in Yugoslavia, but insistence by certain countries such as the Soviet Union and Turkey on the maintenance of the unanimity rule and the need for the governments of the country concerned (e.g. Yugoslavia) to give prior agreement to any action taken, left the organization powerless. The European Community stepped into the breach.

## Political aid

In political terms, the West can provide – and is already providing – considerable help on a bilateral, country-to-country basis to the newly-emerging democracies in Eastern and Central Europe in building up their democratic polities. It is easy to be cynical about that effort because it is not expensive to the country providing it, but this does not mean it is not important: quite the reverse. Such political aid, partly governmental but partly also sponsored by political parties and political foundations in the West, has been concentrated on the Central European 'hopefuls', but has recently been given to the Balkan states too, including Albania, where supervision has been an important aid to the democratic process. Britain has taken a leading part in this effort. Cultural cooperation, including help with education, is also taking place mainly within the framework of bilateral relations. One question, however, remains: who will help the Balkan economies?

## Economic aid

It is quite clear that the task of economic rehabilitation in the Balkans, let alone the whole of ex-communist Europe, is beyond any single country's capacities. The United States, which in 1947–8 extended vital aid to Greece and Turkey under the so-called Truman Doctrine and supported Yugoslavia after its break with Stalin (as well as setting up the gigantic and immensely successful Marshall Plan in Western Europe), can no longer envisage such schemes in these days of large budget deficits. Germany, a long-established trading partner in the region, as well as in Eastern Europe, is likely to remain for some time primarily preoccupied with rehabilitating the former East Germany. Japan, the financial super-power of the 1990s, could become involved but its geographic distance is an important deterrent. The Balkans, like the rest of Eastern and Central Europe, are a job for the multilateral organizations.

Some of them, like the IMF and the World Bank, have already been playing a role in the area (in Yugoslavia, but also in Bulgaria and Romania). When it gets going properly, the London-based European Bank for Reconstruction and Development (EBRD), set up specifically to help the ex-communist countries of Eastern Europe (with their governments' participation), will also have its part to play. It did not start its operations until April 1991 and so it is difficult to judge how effective it will be. Clearly the body with the greatest clout is the European Community. It has had a sort of relationship with communist-ruled Eastern Europe ever since its recognition by the Soviet Union in the mid-1970s.

But it was a distant relationship, except with Yugoslavia. One obstacle to communist countries even applying for membership was always their lack of democratic institutions, a must for EC members. Another was, of course, that they were not economically prepared for the replacement of the command economy by the market one.

The Strasbourg-based Council of Europe, a body uniting not only Nato and EC members but also democratic neutrals in Europe, has been playing an interesting role for some years now, acting as an authority to vet individual countries' democratic credentials. The need for countries wishing to apply for membership of the European Community to obtain, as a precondition for any application, a 'he-is-a-democrat-and-respecter-of-human-rights' certificate from the Council has been a useful norm for European behaviour and an incentive towards pluralism and human rights observance. The need to reassure the Council encouraged the dismantling of military rule in Turkey. In the 1970s and 1980s the Council's democratic conditionality was seen as a useful way of propelling the then still communist-ruled countries in Europe towards political and economic liberalization. Perhaps luckily for the Council and the Community, the fact that these countries were tucked into the Soviet sphere of control meant that the inevitable complications arising out of one or more of them actually fulfilling the conditions and demanding the right to apply for Community membership did not have to be faced.

The sudden collapse of Soviet dominance in Eastern and Central Europe and the election in Central Europe and in Croatia and Slovenia of democratic, non-communist governments have marginalized the Council of Europe, at least in respect of these vetting procedures. The Community has also suddenly been brought face to face with three new sets of problems: first, three credible democratic applicants from Central Europe (Czechoslovakia, Hungary and Poland); second, three applicants with less than fully convincing credentials from the Balkans (Albania, Bulgaria and Romania); and third, an awkward dilemma over Yugoslavia, a country much supported by the Community but now disintegrating amid disorder and violence.

The Community has offered association, or 'Europe Agreements' to Czechoslovakia, Hungary and Poland: in other words, free trade between them and the Community. The offer has been made on the grounds that all three countries have made clear progress towards pluralist democracies and market economies. The three have accepted the offer of negotiations for association but have indicated that what they want eventually is full membership. Negotiations started in December 1990, but it is not at all sure that they will be successfully completed in time to allow for association to come into force by the target date of 1 January 1992. This is not surprising. There are difficulties still to be resolved, particularly over sensitive items such as steel, textiles and of course Central European agricultural exports to the Community.

Both Bulgaria and Romania have expressed a wish for similar Europe Agreements with the Community. The Community's reply has been that it will be necessary to 'monitor closely' their reforms, so that negotiations could begin 'as soon as the necessary conditions have been established'. This formulation suggests that both have a long way to go before serious talking can begin.

In the case of *Bulgaria*, it would probably be well after the association of the three Central European countries. Meanwhile it has its trade and cooperation agreement with the Community to work from as well as its membership of the so-called PHARE* programme. The Community has been charged with the implementation of this programme, launched by the Group of 24 OECD countries (G24) to help former communist states with the transition to political pluralism and the market economy. Among the areas on which the Community has concentrated its technical and financial assistance are privatization and the restructuring of enterprises; the restructuring and modernization of banking and financial services; the promotion of small and medium-sized enterprises and the private sector generally; and labour market agencies and policies, including training.

Bulgaria may also be granted unilateral concessions under the Generalized System of Preferences (GSP) and quota liberalization. The idea is that if the reforms continue successfully, the concessions will be consolidated and the aid increased until, in the fullness of time, Bulgaria moves forward to association with the Community. But, in truth, Bulgaria is to remain on hold for a long time to come.

The same, only more so, applies to *Romania*, which opened its contacts with the Community a long time ago, while still under the Ceausescu regime, even signing a five-year trade and preferential agreement in 1980. The Community hoped that giving Romania trade concessions would enable it to withstand politically-motivated economic pressures from the Soviet Union. Help was suspended for a while in 1990 because of the post-Ceausescu repression. In January 1991, after both Romania's government and its opposition had submitted evidence about the situation in the country to the European Parliament and to the

*Poland and Hungary: aid for economic reconstruction

European Commission in Brussels, the G24 decided that aid should start to flow. But, like Bulgaria, Romania will for a long time be unable to move beyond the PHARE programme and the trade and cooperation agreement.

As far as *Albania* is concerned, the EC took note of the positive changes that occurred in the political and economic situation there after the election on 31 March 1991. That confirmed the ruling Communist Party in power, but a subsequent general strike forced it to form a coalition with the non-communist opposition in May 1991. The EC established diplomatic relations with Albania in June 1991 and in July authorized humanitarian aid to the value of 500,000 ecus to alleviate critical shortages. Meanwhile, Albania's leaders have started lobbying Western governments for support. Senior politicians visited Britain and Italy in May 1991 with some concrete results: diplomatic relations with Britain and the promise of food aid from Italy. The United States authorized urgent humanitarian aid shipments to Albania after a visit to Tirana in June by the Secretary of State, James Baker. Albania is also to be eligible for credits from the EBRD.

*Yugoslavia* has had a long and close relationship with the Community dating back to 1971, when it was granted GSP concessions. The special (and, at the time, unique) agreement signed as a matter of some political urgency in 1980, at the time of President Tito's last illness, gave Yugoslavia a large measure of free entry for its industrial products. This was consolidated during the 1980s so that Yugoslavia enjoyed almost completely free entry, apart from a few quotas on textile products and restrictions on the tariff-free entry of some other products under the GSP. A special protocol provided Yugoslavia with financial assistance from the Community. Under the EC's latest batch of policies towards Eastern Europe, Yugoslavia has received 30m ecus within the framework of the PHARE programme. In effect that has given it, at least in the short term, most of what the Central Europeans are likely to get under their Europe Agreements.

However, the main question mark now is not so much over the finer technicalities of the next stage of Yugoslavia's relationship with the EC, but over the future of the state itself. In June 1991, when Croatia and Slovenia declared their independence, they simultaneously announced their intention of joining the Community eventually as separate states (at present, the Community works with the republics but through the central government). The Community has at regular intervals – notably at the European Council on 28 October 1990 but also subsequently – reiterated its well-known and oft-stated preference for the 'preservation of the unity and territorial integrity of Yugoslavia'. This was the message to all in Yugoslavia from the senior EC mission in June 1991 led by Jacques Delors, the President of the European Commission. First Slovenia's and Croatia's declaration of independence, and then the Yugoslav army's attempt to secure Slovenia's borders by force faced the Community with a challenge to revise its policy towards Yugoslavia.

A change in that policy had clearly been called for. The 'head-in-the-sand' policy of sticking to Yugoslavia come what may had clearly become inadequate to cope with the new reality. Besides, the Community was offering encouragement to the centralist forces by its insistence on a united Yugoslavia and warnings uttered at various times, particularly by the Italian Foreign Minister, Gianni de Michelis, that Croatia and Slovenia would face a cold welcome if they went ahead with their plans for independence. The Community responded to the army's attack on Slovenia by dispatching no fewer than three ministerial 'troikas': the first headed by Luxembourg's Foreign Minister, and then after 1 July (when the Netherlands assumed the presidency of the European Council) by the Dutch Foreign Minister. The ceasefires negotiated by the first two troikas collapsed, but the third, negotiated at talks lasting 16 hours on the island of Brioni, formerly President Tito's residence, came into effect on 7 July and has so far held. In accordance with the agreement between the EC mission and Croat, Slovene and federal Yugoslav leaders, the Yugoslav army began to withdraw to its barracks in Slovenia, as did the Slovene territorial forces that had been fighting them. The Yugoslav army was allowed to resume control of the frontier area. The Croat and Slovene parliaments ratified the agreement, which also included provisions for EC monitors to supervise the ceasefire until talks about the future of Yugoslavia began on 1 August.

It remained to be seen how the Yugoslav army and Serbia would respond to EC monitors being sent to areas of Croatia where an insurrection by Serb irregular forces had been in progress since August 1990. The Community concentrated first on seeing the relatively simpler problem of Slovenia to a peaceful solution but in July grasped the nettle of conflict in Croatia by dispatching another 'troika' mission and greatly increasing the number of monitors there.

All this represented a welcome and overdue change in EC policy but the issue of the possible recognition of Slovenia and Croatia remained unresolved owing to Franco–German differences, France being against and Germany in favour of recognition.

By acting as it did, however belatedly, the Community made a constructive contribution to the resolution of the Yugoslav crisis, and also sent an important and encouraging signal to the whole region. But its main focus of interest will remain, as before, in Central Europe, not the Balkans, however much atention may be claimed by Yugoslavia now.

## Friends and neighbours

Rescue for the hard-pressed Balkans should be both a long-term and a short-term attempt. As Western governments and institutions adjust their Balkan policy to the Yugoslav challenge and its consequences, an important role in the short-term salvation of the Balkans can also be played by countries like Austria, Greece and Italy. They qualify for the task by virtue both of their geographical proximity and of their economic and security interests in the area. Dealing with the biggest problem in the Balkans today – Yugoslavia's dissolution – will, however, involve all of its neighbours, the better-off ones as well as those which are themselves in need of assistance.

Fortunately, unlike in the pre-1941 period, there are at the moment no vultures perched on Yugoslavia's borders, waiting to pounce on the federation's decomposing body to grab their pound of flesh. A more apt image to describe Yugoslavia's neighbours is that of worried tenants in an apartment house, who have already lost a lot of sleep because of a 'mother of all rows' at one of the apartments, that sounds as if it could at any moment spill over on to the landings and staircases. Humanity but also self-interest inspires them to offer cups of tea, or possibly something stronger, to the inhabitants of the disturbed apartment.

Only the bare outlines of this good-neighbourly activity, which also allows glimpses of possible new future Balkan alliances, are visible at the moment. Like the Western governments and the Community, Yugoslavia's neighbours must act tactfully, observing diplomatic niceties and, above all, avoiding taking sides openly. But they have been acting, all the same.

### Austria

Austria, for which the old Habsburg connection as well as geographical proximity are important factors, has so far shown the greatest readiness to help Croatia and Slovenia as they disengage from Yugoslavia. Even before the war in Slovenia it had allowed discussions about linking the Austrian schilling with the new Slovene and Croat currencies that would replace the Yugoslav dinar after independence. A tactless invitation by an Austrian right-wing politician to Slovenia to 'become Austria's tenth *Land*' has ruffled a few feathers among the Slovenes, but without dampening their enthusiasm for the Austrian connection. The generous moral support to Slovenia in its war with the Yugoslav army by both the Austrian government and its people has created a new bond.

It remains to be seen what long-term impact Austria's close links with Slovenia and Croatia will have on its application to join the Community. Acting as a helpful minder for hopeful aspirants likely to be condemned to a long period of waiting could be considered an indirect service for the Community and thus boost Austria's standing in Brussels. Meanwhile, a connection that opens up new trading and other opportunities cannot do Austria any harm. The economic motive behind Austria's *Südostpolitik* is clearly visible in the cooperation Austria's *Länder* are pursuing with Croatia, Slovenia and other members of the Alpen-Adria regional 'working community', whose current chairman is Upper Austria.

## Hungary

Like Yugoslavia's other neighbours, Hungary faces special dilemmas, connected with its concern for its minorities abroad, in responding to the new reality developing in Yugoslavia. For decades now, Hungary has regarded the Yugoslav federal framework as satisfactory for the country's Hungarian minority, nearly half-a-million strong and mainly situated in Vojvodina. Until the late 1980s, the treatment of the Hungarian minority in Yugoslavia was far more liberal than in Romania or even Czechoslovakia. The present, well-founded fear in Budapest is that, in an independent, strongly nationalistic Serbia containing Vojvodina, the Hungarian minority's position could become more exposed than in a broader, ethnically more varied and balanced Yugoslavia. But Hungary, realizing that it has no power to influence the situation in Yugoslavia, follows a double strategy.

On the one hand, it tries to keep on terms with Serbia. This has proved difficult, not least because of the growing Serbian nationalistic pressure on the Vojvodina Hungarians since the pro-Milosevic regime came to power in the province in the autumn of 1988. As the situation in Yugoslavia continued to deteriorate in the summer of 1991, the Hungarian government issued a warning to Serbia that it could not remain indifferent to the adverse effects on its minority in Vojvodina caused by changes in internal borders. On the other hand, Hungary has been developing, with much greater success, close relations with Slovenia and Croatia, whose top leaders have been received at the highest level in Hungary.

The sale of light arms in the autumn of 1990 to the Croat government for its new gendarmerie has proved far more controversial. It has exposed the Budapest government to accusations from Serbia of interference in Yugoslavia's domestic affairs. Hungary's domestic opposition has exploited the episode to attack the coalition government, in which the Hungarian Democratic Forum is the main element. Ideological closeness has helped foster good relations with Slovenia and Croatia, both of which elected in the spring of 1990 right-of-centre governments similar in outlook to the Hungarian Democratic Forum.

Ideology may be a bond, but – like Austria – land-locked Hungary also has a strong economic interest in developing closer links with both Croatia and Slovenia. An important element of that cooperation could be the so-called Adria pipeline, which dates back to the era of cheap oil before 1973. Little used for more than a decade, it has become topical again because of Hungary's need to diversify its oil imports in view of the reduced Soviet deliveries to Central Europe. Adriatic ports are also of interest, notably the big port of Rijeka in Croatia, familiar (as Fiume) to the Hungarians from the pre-1918 period as an important trade outlet.

## Italy

Italy, under its Socialist Foreign Minister, Gianni de Michelis, has produced a number of schemes, in each of which a united Yugoslavia forms a key element. This was not accidental: de Michelis has been a strong supporter of Yugoslavia in public as well as an influential voice in its favour behind the scenes in EC councils. Italy's support for Yugoslavia has been based on the perception (derived from historical experience) that it is easier to do business with – and obtain concessions from – a strong government in Belgrade than those in Zagreb and Ljubljana. It is of course easier, when it comes to accommodating Italy's aspirations and interests in the Adriatic region, for the more distant (and therefore also more relaxed) Serbs to be cooperative than for the Croats and the Slovenes, who are right next door to Italy and ready to defend every inch of their coast and every island, however small.

Another factor in Italy's thinking about Yugoslavia's dissolution is the possibility that it might set a precedent for and encourage demands by the German-speaking population in Alto Adige/South Tyrol to rejoin Austria. And finally, as already indicated, Italy fears a large refugee influx if Yugoslavia were to break up amid disorder and civil war. Those fears have been reinforced by the Albanian exodus to Italy in 1990–91.

But, like the other governments of the region, Italy takes a pragmatic view of the Yugoslav situation and will recognize realities when it has to: whether a loose confederation (now increasingly unlikely) or, if need be, a total break-up. Meanwhile, Italy has been quietly developing close contacts, through its consulates in Zagreb and Ljubljana, with the governments of Croatia and Slovenia. For a number of years, four northern Italian regions have been cooperating in an unspectacular but useful way within the framework of the Alpen–Adria 'working community'.

A more ambitious, chiefly Italian, project for the region is the so-called *Pentagonale* grouping. This was launched first in 1989 as the *Quadrilaterale*, and included Austria, Hungary, Italy and Yugoslavia; Czechoslovakia was a later addition. Poland joined in July 1991, making it the *Hexagonale*. Politically, it was a bid by the Italians for leadership of Central Europe, behind which lay their fears of German dominance in both Central and southern Europe. Austria welcomed the *Pentagonale* as an extension of the good work begun by the more modest Alpen–Adria grouping, and as a useful link with Czechoslovakia. The Czechoslovak President, Vaclav Havel, has shown keen personal interest in the political aspects of this plan, whereas Hungary and Yugoslavia have been chiefly interested in the possibilities the framework seems to offer for the regional infrastructure, especially in transport and energy. But these plans have continued to hang fire owing to the uncertain fate of Yugoslavia, a key link in the prospective grouping.

In April 1991 Italy launched another regional plan for a Mediterranean regional community to include Italy's southern regions, Albania, Greece, Serbia, Montenegro, Croatia and – as an observer – Slovenia. The aim of the scheme is cooperation in the northern Mediterranean, which would ensure greater regional stability, a key Italian concern. It remains to be seen whether this plan will actually get off the ground. If it does, it could, among other things, provide a useful framework for Italy and Greece to help Albania economically.

### Romania

Romania has shown a keen interest in developing close relations with Serbia. This is partly a reflection of strong common economic interests (hydroelectric power stations on the Danube, cooperation in arms production with the Yugoslav army, and other joint projects); and partly, too, a reflection of the ideological closeness between Ion Iliescu and Slobodan Milosevic, both populist communist leaders.

The fact that both Serbia and Romania have sizeable and vocal

Hungarian minorities – though Romania's is much larger than Serbia's – is also a common bond. Romania, whose international isolation is due to a large extent to its repressive policy towards its Hungarian minority, appreciates close relations with Serbia, which has also provoked international criticism because of its repressive policy towards the Albanians in Kosovo (as well as, more recently, towards the Hungarians in Vojvodina). Romania and Serbia share enough old traditions and present interests to ensure that a close relationship between the two states will survive even the current neo-communist regime. Although the friendship with Serbia has helped to lessen Romania's sense of international isolation, that isolation is not absolute: outside the Balkans, Romania enjoys some backing from the Latin bloc in Europe – France, Italy and Spain.

## Greece

Greece has a close interest in the fate of its national minority in southern Albania but no official territorial claims there. However, there are irredentist figures in Greece such as Archbishop Sevastianos in Konitsa in Epirus, a supporter of the so-called Movement for the Recovery of Vorio Epirus, who is campaigning for the implementation of the 1914 Protocol of Corfu, which gave northern Epirus to Greece but was revoked by the 1921 Ambassadors' Conference. This sort of talk gives the notoriously suspicious Albanians at least some grounds for believing that, if civil war broke out in Albania, thus emphasizing regional differences, Greece might be interested in the dismemberment of their country.

Greece worries about the break-up of Yugoslavia for practical reasons such as the threat that civil disorder in Yugoslavia poses to Greece's commercially important transit routes through that country. Even more important, it is hostile towards the prospect of an independent Macedonia under a nationalist government with a mission to unite all Macedonians – including those in Greece whose existence Greece denies, as well as those in Bulgaria whose existence Bulgaria denies. It should not be forgotten – and the Greeks will not forget it for a long time – that the ruinous civil war in the late 1940s and early 1950s had been waged by the Greek communists from bases in Yugoslav Macedonia and that the insurgent Greek communist units of General Markos had contained a large number of people regarding themselves as ethnic Macedonians. After their defeat, many of these 'Slavophones'(Greek Macedonians) were obliged to take refuge in various East European countries. This was one of the factors that helped to reduce the Slav minority in Greece, which had already been diminished by the voluntary exchange of populations with Bulgaria under the Treaty of Neuilly in 1919.

Greece's common front with Bulgaria over Macedonia was manifested during a visit to Athens in March 1991 of the Bulgarian Prime Minister, Dimitar Popov, when he and the Greek Prime Minister, Constantine Mitsotakis, issued a statement denying the existence of ethnic minorities on their respective territories. The visit to Greece in April 1991 by Serbia's President, Slobodan Milosevic, during which he was treated by Greece's conservative government as a head of state, confirmed the widespread impression that Serbia was regarded by Greece as a valuable ally vis-à-vis both Macedonia and Albania.

For Greece, even more pressing than its security concerns in the western Balkans is its troubled unequal relationship with its fellow-member in Nato, Turkey, which many Greeks see as a modern version of the Ottoman empire and as a direct threat. Several disputes, including that over Cyprus, divide Greece and Turkey, but behind it all lies the Greeks' awareness of their country's weakness in relation to the 'colossus on the Bosporus'.

Both Greece and Bulgaria see Turkey as a potential threat. In addition, both have Muslim minorities which they fear Turkey will increasingly want to take under its wing. Both these factors help account for the close relationship between the two countries that began in the late 1960s while Bulgaria was still under the communists and Greece under the colonels, and that has developed over the years. Greece gave Bulgaria some food aid during the difficult 1990–91 winter, including a gift of 15,000 tons of oranges and other citrus fruit in January 1991. But Greece has some real economic interests in Bulgaria and has lately been considering the increased use of transport routes through Bulgaria and then direct through Serbia, thus avoiding Macedonia. Greek road traffic has been disrupted repeatedly since 1989 by political strikes in Yugoslav Macedonia in support of Greece's ethnic Macedonians. Bulgaria hopes that Greece will speak up for it in the European Community and generally help it by credits and private investment. Whether these hopes will be fulfilled will depend on how successfully the present weaknesses in the Greek economy are overcome.

### Bulgaria

It is vitally important for Bulgaria to maintain, for the foreseeable future, its trade with the Soviet Union, which supplies the bulk of its energy requirements. Given its current desperate straits, sheer economic survival is the principal preoccupation of Bulgaria, both government and people. But the Bulgarians exhibit signs of nervousness about the break-up of Yugoslavia. The prospect of Macedonia, for decades the cherished national goal, becoming detached from Yugoslavia and, in principle at least, free to join Bulgaria, evokes not joy but anxiety, particularly among politicians. In their eyes (though they could not admit it in public) the impoverished Macedonia, with its large Albanian population, does not look like a desirable acquisition but rather a headache to be shared – with Greece, in the first place, which is similarly dismayed by the unfolding of events in Yugoslavia.

The Bulgarians reckon that Greece would not, at the moment at any rate, look kindly upon Macedonia's union with their country. Bulgaria cannot afford to quarrel with Greece or cross it. For one thing, as we have seen, the Bulgarians would like Greece to plead their case over EC association and, in the fullness of time, membership. Moreover, in security terms, the Greek connection is a safeguard for Bulgaria against Turkey, a powerful neighbour that – although not contemplating a reconquest of territories of the former Ottoman empire – is certain to retain an inconveniently close interest in the fate of Bulgaria's Muslim minority.

Given those problems, an acceptable solution of the Macedonian question, from the Bulgarian point of view, could be an independent Macedonia under a leadership ready to accept its present borders within Yugoslavia as final, to renounce any territorial aspirations towards either Bulgaria or Greece, and to promise not to act as a protector for any Macedonians living in those two states. However, it is quite possible that if an independent Macedonia on its own did not prove ultimately to be a viable state, its most likely final home would, after all, be Bulgaria. But this could represent a stable solution only if it were approved by a referendum of the Macedonian and Bulgarian peoples and within a broader Balkan consensus. In other words, it would need the consent of Bulgaria's neighbours, Greece and Serbia, as well as Albania.

*Albania*

Albania has never encouraged secession in the Kosovo province, contrary to frequent accusations of interference from Yugoslavia. Also, it has given only verbal support to the Kosovo Albanians' unsuccessful demand for greater autonomy (as in their 1981 demonstrations for a republic within Yugoslavia on a par with Serbia, Croatia and the others). Clearly, power was to Enver Hoxha always more important than a foreign policy adventure likely to provoke not only armed conflict with a stronger (and internationally popular) neighbour but also possible internal turmoil in Albania itself, that might endanger his position. Persistent claims by Belgrade of alleged 'Tirana-inspired irredentism' never had any substance to them and were meant for domestic consumption.

But the political upheaval in Albania during 1990–91 that led to multi-party elections, the emergence of a functioning opposition, a coalition government of communists and non-communists, and increased foreign contacts will all have important consequences for the situation in Kosovo too. There have been contacts between Kosovo's ethnic Albanian politicians and both the opposition and the government in Tirana. Significantly, for the first time it is easier for Albanians from Albania to visit Kosovo than vice versa. The government in Tirana realizes that it has got to do more for its fellow-Albanians than complain about their oppression in Yugoslavia, but its difficulty is to know exactly what to do without encouraging a dangerous general uprising. That could happen, anyway, and sooner than many people outside expect, and would pose difficult dilemmas for both the government and the opposition.

The combination of the political opening in Albania and the closing-off of the recent Albanian hopes of autonomy in Yugoslavia has united the three and a half million Albanians in Albania and the two and a half million in Yugoslavia. With Yugoslavia crumbling, the prospect of a Greater Albania has at last become a possibility for the first time since 1945 – although this does not mean it is likely, at least for some time: much would still have to change in the neighbourhood, and within Albania itself. Ironically, one of the most significant single factors that helped to make the prospect real has been the Greater Serbian (and strongly anti-Albanian) offensive under Slobodan Milosevic. This has fatally weakened the Yugoslav state and at the same time united Kosovo's Albanians in opposition to it and made them incline towards union with Albania. A strong, cohesive Yugoslavia could probably have continued to hang on to Kosovo indefinitely. Serbia's attempt to do so will ultimately fail. In a longer historical perspective, Kosovo's union with Albania seems inevitable, although it will not happen without a struggle with Serbia, possibly even a Serbian attempt to prevent the loss of Kosovo by a pre-emptive strike against a still rather weak Albania.

**Networks for the new millennium**

Regional groupings are likely to assume an ever greater importance in Europe during the rest of the 1990s and beyond. It is possible to discern the shape of two such groupings in south-eastern Europe, each bound together by tradition and common economic and security interests but also linked to others in the neighbourhood and within the broader European context. These groupings will comprise sovereign states getting together not to build Berlin or Chinese walls to keep others out, but forging links to neighbours and others beyond in customs unions, free-trade areas and so on. One of the functions of powerful outsiders could be to foster this openness and discourage inward-looking tendencies.

In the west could be a loose grouping of (mainly) Catholic states, those which had once been part of the Habsburg empire – a *Kleinmitteleuropa* (Little Central Europe) bound together by tradition but, even more, by perceived common economic and security interests and linked – together or separately – to other states and groupings, including the European Community. Its members could be Austria, Bosnia (a Habsburg land between 1878 and 1918), Czechoslovakia (either as the federal state it is now or as its two halves), Croatia, Hungary and Slovenia. Italy, too big perhaps to be fully or directly involved in such a combination of states, could play the role of a benevolent big neighbour, with a strong economic interest in developing closer links with this grouping.

To the east could be a grouping of states – call it a Balkan confederation, or perhaps *Balkania* – sharing the Orthodox tradition and cooperating in the economic field (here, in particular, the existing Balkan cooperation machinery set up at the 1988 Balkan states conference and developed since could be extremely useful). This grouping could include Bulgaria, Greece, Montenegro, Romania and Serbia, with Macedonia in the middle as an independent state or perhaps, ultimately, a part of Bulgaria – should Greece and Serbia permit and the Macedonians despair of a future on their own.

Albania could be associated with this grouping from the start, not least because such an association could perhaps provide a framework for a gradual solution – or at least for a defusing – of the explosive Kosovo issue that divides Serbia and Albania. But Kosovo represents perhaps the knottiest problem in the whole of the Balkans today and may be incapable of resolution without a further and dangerous contest between the forces involved.

Turkey, if it feels so inclined, could eventually become associated with the Balkan grouping, although there would be some initial fear that it would assume a hegemonic position. But whether from within or from the outside, Turkey could fulfil a useful role by taking an interest in

Albania, as it has already started doing. It could thus match anything its other neighbours, notably Italy, might be able to do to support it politically and economically. Turkish backing for Albania would help to deter those in Greece and Serbia who may still be dreaming of carving Albania up between them. The same is true of Macedonia, if Turkey could be induced to show an interest in supporting it. Interestingly, the first foreign visit of Macedonia's new president, Kiro Gligorov, was to Ankara, in July 1991.

States usually cooperate and unite in common action not only for positive but also for negative reasons – against somebody or for want of opportunity of joining a better club. Every ex-communist state in the Balkans wants to 'join Europe' – just as the ex-communist states further north do. But the wait, particularly for full membership of the Community, could be very long. Meanwhile, there could be disappointment with the norms of today – full free marketry and political pluralism – and a search for different formulas. The good thing about such groupings as might be emerging in the Balkans now is that they would be flexible enough to fulfil many different purposes and roles for their various members.

Realistically speaking, the *Kleinmitteleuropa* grouping could link its members more closely to 'Europe' but it could also be a shield against both future German hegemony in the north and possible local irredentist moves from, say, Italy in the west and Serbia in the east. Last but not least, it could help to deter a resurgent Soviet Union from trying to muscle in on the Balkans one day. A Balkan confederation could, in a sense, do even more. Psychologically, it could offer its more defensively-minded members a measure of reassurance against both Catholicism and Islam (defined as broad politico-religious tendencies). More specifically, Serbia could feel reassured against what is these days seen among the Serbs as the Albanian demographic wave rolling northwards and 'engulfing' their country. Bulgaria, Greece and Serbia would be able, within such a framework, to accept a separate Macedonia. For both Greece and Bulgaria, there would be an additional reassurance in such company against fears of Turkish hegemony over the region. (Such fears, including current talk both in Bulgaria and in Greece, of a 'hundred million strong neo-Ottoman Islamic empire', may be – and probably are – unrealistic, but *Angst* is the stuff of politics in the Balkans as much as elsewhere.) As far as Romania is concerned, membership of such a Balkan grouping would take it out of its isolation from its neighbours and the rest of Europe and, very important, prevent over-dependence on

Russia. The Turkish scheme for Black Sea Cooperation, taking in all the states concerned – Bulgaria, Romania, the Soviet Union and of course Turkey itself – and signed in July 1991, is partly designed to allay the mutual fears of these states.

*Kleinmitteleuropa* and a Balkan confederation: a speculative scheme, admittedly, but perhaps with an element of realism in it. And if it resembles the pattern of those pre-1914 alliances, then it does so only very superficially and with one vital difference: because of the strategic downgrading of the Balkans, there is no danger this time of another world war; but also, regrettably, there will be no absolutely firm promise of local peace either. Kosovo's continuing occupation by Serbia and the strong possibility of an uprising by the desperate ethnic Albanian majority there, eventually involving Albania itself, could provide the spark for a local conflagration every bit as nasty as, and probably far more serious than, the present conflict in the western and central parts of the dissolving Yugoslav federation.

*Im Balkan viel Neues.* Things have certainly changed in the Balkans, but have they changed for the better? The post-communist order is still in the making but there is no need to cry for the *Pax Sovietica*, a lost half-century for the region. Acquisition of territory, for one thing, has ceased to be the consuming preoccupation it once was. Good economic performance is appreciated as what makes states strong and stable. Although Yugoslavia's acceptance of that principle must await the resolution of the current messy but necessary reordering process, it is a principle that is coming to be understood by the new post-communist leaders, as well as their peoples, and will perhaps in the end encourage cooperation rather than irredentist wars.

# NOTES

1 For an up-to-date treatment of Turkey as a Middle Eastern power, see Philip
  Robins, *Turkey and the Middle East* (Chatham House Papers, RIIA/Pinter,
  May 1991).
2 Karl Marx and Friedrich Engels, *Manifesto of the Communist Party*, English
  translation annotated by Friedrich Engels (New York: International
  Publishers, 1932), p. 28.
3 V. I. Lenin, 'Critical Remarks on the National Question', in *Questions of
  National Policy and Proletarian Internationalism* (Moscow: Progress
  Books, n.d.), p. 30.
4 Svetozar Vukmanovic-Tempo, *Revolucija koja tece: Memoari* (Belgrade:
  Komunist, 1971), vol. I, p. 30.
5 For a full and authoritative account of Albanian conflicts during World War
  II, see Sir Reginald Hibbert, *The Bitter Victory: Albania's National
  Liberation Struggle* (London: Pinter, 1991). The author was in Albania
  during World War II as an officer working for the Special Operations
  Executive (SOE).
6 The extremely complex and controversial question of the exact number of
  people – Serbs, Croats, Jews, Muslims and others – killed in Yugoslavia
  during World War II is treated seriously and with remarkable objectivity in
  two studies, one by a Serb and one by a Croat. The Serb author, who has
  lived in the West for many years, is Bogoljub Kocovic. His book, published
  by *Nasa Rec*, a Serbian monthly, in London in 1985, is called *Zrtve drugog
  svetskog rata u Jugoslaviji* ('Victims of the Second World War in Yugoslavia'). The author of the other study, called *Gubici stanovnistva u drugom
  svjetskom ratu* ('Losses of the Population of Yugoslavia in the Second
  World War'), is a population expert, Professor Vladimir Zerjavic. His study
  was published in Zagreb by the Yugoslav Victimological Society with the

support of the Jewish community in Zagreb. Both Kocovic and Zerjavic come to remarkably similar conclusions, even though they carried out their research independently of each other. Both state that the actual figure was, fortunately, much lower than the 1.7m frequently quoted.

7 For the 'revisionist', pro-Mihailovic view, see Michael Lees, *The Rape of Serbia: The British Role in Tito's Grab for Power 1943–1944* (New York: Harcourt Brace Jovanovich, 1990); and David Martin, *The Web of Disinformation: Churchill's Yugoslav Blunder* (New York: Harcourt Brace Jovanovich, 1990). Still the best scholarly work on Mihailovic's movement is Jozo Tomasevich, *The Chetniks* (Stanford, CA: Stanford University Press, 1975).

8 See Richard Crampton, *A Short History of Modern Bulgaria* (Cambridge: Cambridge University Press, 1987), pp. 148–9.

9 That understanding, scribbled on a piece of paper by Churchill and ticked by Stalin, gave the Soviet Union a 90% stake in Romania and 75% in Bulgaria, while Britain (and the West in general) got 90% in Greece. Each side received a 50% stake in Hungary and in Yugoslavia. See Winston Churchill, *The Second World War, Vol. 11: The Tide of Victory* (London: Cassell, 1954, paperback edition 1964), pp. 200–1.

10 For a fuller treatment of the competing railways question, see Orme Wilson Jr.,'The Belgrade-Bar Railway: An Essay in Economic and Political Geography', in George W. Hoffman, ed., *Eastern Europe: Essays in Geographical Problems* (London: Methuen, 1971), pp. 365–94.

11 Much has been written on the subject of Yugoslav self-management, most of it rather unilluminating or even positively misleading. One of the few who saw through the obfuscations was Ljubo Sirc in *The Yugoslav Economy under Self-Management* (London: Macmillan, 1979).

12 See Dusan Bilandzic, *Jugoslavija poslije Tita 1980–1985* (Zagreb: Globus, 1987).

13 The 1981 census figures mentioned in this chapter are available in *Statisticki godisnjak Jugoslavije 1988* (Belgrade: Savezni zavod za statistiku, 1988).

14 The first full published version of the Memorandum appeared in the Zagreb journal *Nase teme*, Nos. 1–2/1989. A book that expresses the essence of Serbian feelings about Yugoslavia and the Serbs' position in it is Danko Popovic's best-seller *Knjiga o Milutinu* (Belgrade: Knjizevne Novine, 1985).

15 Branko Horvat, *Kosovsko pitanje* (Zagreb: Globus, 1988).

16 *Borba* (Belgrade), 11 July 1991.

# BIBLIOGRAPHICAL NOTE

It is not practicable in a short work such as this to provide more than a few references to sources used in the course of its preparation – let alone an exhaustive bibliography. But here are a few suggestions (to supplement those works cited in the Notes) for readers who may wish to explore further certain of the themes covered.

Still the most comprehensive general manual on Eastern Europe, with a lot of historical background, is *The Soviet Union and Eastern Europe*, edited by George Schöpflin (London: Muller, Blond and White, 1986, second edition, 637 pages). The two best and most up-to-date general surveys of the recent history of Eastern and Central Europe, both by Joseph Rothschild, are: *East Central Europe between the Two World Wars* (Seattle and London: University of Washington Press, 1974, 420 pages); and *Return to Diversity: A Political History of East Central Europe since World War II* (New York and Oxford: Oxford University Press, 1989, 257 pages). Another concise, useful work covering the whole region is Antony Polonsky's *The Little Dictators: The History of Eastern Europe since 1918* (London and Boston: Routledge and Kegan Paul, 1975, 212 pages).

For a feel of what Europe – and Eastern Europe, in particular – was like in the pre-communist era, it pays to dip into John Gunter's splendid *Inside Europe* (London: Hamish Hamilton, 1936). In the section on Yugoslavia, for example, it reports that 'General Goering swooped on a few visits to Yugoslavia and pleased the boy King with a tremendous toy railway as a birthday gift'.

Specifically on the Balkans, there are two useful works: Barbara Jelavich's *History of the Balkans, Vol. 2: Twentieth Century* (Cambridge: Cambridge University Press, 1984, 647 pages); and the volume edited by Charles and Barbara Jelavich, *The Balkans in Transition: Essays on the Development of Balkan Life and Politics since the Eighteenth Century* (Berkeley and Los Angeles: University of California Press, 1963, 451 pages). The often neglected but

111

important economic angle is treated in a joint work by John R. Lampe and Marvin R. Jackson, *Balkan Economic History 1550–1950: From Imperial Borderlands to Developing Nations* (Bloomington: Indiana University Press, 1982, 728 pages). A useful volume looking at contemporary conflicts in the Balkans from a historical perspective is *Problems of Balkan Security: Southeastern Europe in the 1990s*, edited by Paul S. Shoup (Project Director: George W. Hoffman) and published by the Wilson Centre Press in Washington in 1990.

The most acute and perceptive analysis of the relationship between communism and nationalism in the Balkans, still topical and valid despite having been published two decades ago, is Paul Lendvai's *Eagles in Cobwebs* (London: Macdonald, 1970, 396 pages). In the same category of works published long ago but still illuminating is Elisabeth Barker's short study *Macedonia: Its Place in Balkan Power Politics* (London: Royal Institute of International Affairs, 1950, reprinted 1980, 129 pages). Macedonia is also the subject of a joint work by Stephen E. Palmer Jr. and Robert R. King, *Yugoslav Communism and the Macedonian Question* (Hamden: Archon Books, 1971, 247 pages).

A helpful work providing a broader conceptual framework for thinking about nationalism is Anthony D. Smith's *National Identity* (Harmondsworth: Penguin Books, 1991, 227 pages). It is interesting to read it in conjunction with an early attempt to make sense of the whole problem of nationalism, a study compiled by a team at Chatham House in the 1930s under the chairmanship of E. H. Carr. Its title was *Nationalism* and it was published by Oxford University Press for the RIIA in 1939.

The main Balkan disputes are treated in some detail in the Robert R. King's well-documented scholarly study *Minorities under Communism: Nationalities as a Source of Tension among Balkan Communist States* (Harvard: Harvard University Press, 1973). An up-to-date treatment of the minorities issue is to be found in *The Balkans: Minorities and States in Conflict*, by Hugh Poulton (London: Minority Rights Publications, 244 pages).

*Albania*. The most thoroughly researched and best-written study, with a wealth of contemporary material and a sense of perspective, is Anton Logoreci's *The Albanians: Europe's Forgotten Survivors* (London: Gollancz, 1977, 230 pages). Also useful is Peter R. Profti's *Socialist Albania since 1944: Domestic and Foreign Developments* (Cambridge, MA: The MIT Press, 1978, 311 pages).

*Bulgaria*. The best overall study, concise and informative, is Richard Crampton's *A Short History of Modern Bulgaria* (Cambridge: Cambridge University Press, 1987, 221 pages). For the crucial early period of communist power, there is J. F. Brown's *Bulgaria under Communist Rule* (London: Praeger, 1970, 339 pages).

*Romania*. The most useful works are, for the early communist period, Ghita Ionescu's *Communism in Rumania, 1944–1962* (London: Oxford University Press, 1964, 378 pages); and for the Ceausescu era, Michael Shafir's *Romania: Politics, Economics, Society: Political Stagnation and Simulated Change* (London: Pinter, 1985, 232 pages).

*Yugoslavia.* The key work for understanding the whole of the Yugoslav problem is Ivo Banac's magnificent monograph *The National Question in Yugoslavia: Origins, History, Politics* (Ithaca and London: Cornell University Press, 1984, 452 pages). The national factor within the Communist Party is the subject of his *With Stalin Against Tito: Cominformist Splits in Yugoslav Communism* (Ithaca and London: Cornell University Press, 1988, 294 pages). A very good monograph on the same subject is Paul Shoup's *Communism and the Yugoslav National Question* (New York and London: Columbia Viking Press, 1968, 308 pages). A lucid, comprehensive survey of the Tito period is Sir Duncan Wilson's work *Tito's Yugoslavia* (Cambridge: Cambridge University Press, 1979, 269 pages). A useful concise compendium is a volume originally prepared for the Naval Intelligence Division during World War II and updated and edited by Stephen Clissold, *A Short History of Yugoslavia: From Early Times to 1966* (Cambridge: Cambridge University Press, 1966, 279 pages). Stephen Clissold also edited a selection of documents, prefaced with a long, illuminating essay and called *Yugoslavia and the Soviet Union 1939–1973*. It was published by Oxford University Press for the Royal Institute of International Affairs in 1975.

# Also in this series

## East Central Europe from Reform to Transformation
### Judy Batt

This book provides a concise account of the breakdown of communist rule in Poland, Hungary and Czechoslovakia and a comparative analysis of the problems and prospects of their transition to pluralist democratic politics and market economies. A major theme is the linkage of politics and economics: the book shows how both the failure of economic reforms in Poland and Hungary and the resistance to economic reform in Czechoslovakia contributed to undermining the communist monopoly of power; and how the new politics of multi-party pluralism of the post-communist era interact with the unprecedented task of radical economic transformation.

## Contents

1 Economic reform in the crisis of communist rule
2 The end of communist rule
3 The emergence of pluralist politics
4 The politics of economic transformation

## The author

Judy Batt is a Lecturer in Soviet and East European Politics at the Centre for Russian and East European Studies, University of Birmingham, and an Associate Fellow of the Royal Institute of International Affairs.

RIIA/PINTER PUBLISHERS

## The European Community and Eastern Europe
### John Pinder

Economic reforms and new policies in both Western and Eastern Europe have stimulated a debate on how best to restructure the relationships between them through association and possible enlargement of the European Community. This paper surveys the emerging patterns of trade, economic cooperation and financial links. It examines both the economic interests and instruments of the European Community and the political options. These issues are assessed in the light of *perestroika* in the Soviet Union and reforms in Eastern Europe.

### Contents

### The author

John Pinder is a member of the Council of the Royal Institute of International Affairs and was formerly Director of the Policy Studies Institute. His publications include *The Economies of Europe* (1971), *The European Community's Policy towards Eastern Europe* (with Pauline Pinder, 1975), and many other contributions on the EC and on relations with Eastern Europe.

## RIIA/PINTER PUBLISHERS

# Also in this series

## Turkey and the Middle East
### *Philip Robins*

Turkey's importance in the Middle East increased steadily as the Gulf crisis of 1990-91 developed. However, its potential as a major actor in Middle Eastern affairs has been largely overlooked because of its persistent desire to play a role in Europe. This study begins by assessing the effect of political currents in the region on the internal politics of Turkey, and then proceeds to examine Turkish interests and ambitions in the context of the continuing Arab-Israeli dispute, the Gulf conflict during the 1980s and the 1990 Iraqi invasion of Kuwait. Turkey's economic relations with the Middle Eastern countries are also treated in detail. Finally, the study considers Turkey's future political, economic and strategic role in the Middle East, arguing that it needs greater recognition and greater integration in international affairs.

## Contents

## The author

Dr Philip Robins is head of the Middle East Programme at the Royal Institute of International Affairs. He has written widely on Iraq, Jordan and the Gulf, and appeared frequently on radio and television during the Gulf crisis in 1990-91. Previously he worked at the Economist Intelligence Unit, and as a journalist based in the Middle East.

## RIIA/PINTER PUBLISHERS

## CHATHAM HOUSE PAPERS

# Also in this series

## The Transformation of
## Western Europe

### *William Wallace*

Western Europe has undergone dramatic changes in the 40 years since European integration was launched. The institutions set up in the postwar years - OEEC/OECD, the Council of Europe, NATO, WEU, above all the European Communities - have set the framework for relations among the West European governments since the 1950s. Yet the character of the European economy has been transformed by industrial integration and technical change. The revolution in communications has created a European society, moving across national borders and responding to shared information. The security umbrella provided by the Americans against the Soviet threat has become less central. This study looks at the interaction of political, security, economic and social developments since the European Communities were founded, notes the magnetic attraction of an integrating Western Europe for a widening circle of countries, and draws conclusions from these past trends for Europe's likely future development.

## Contents

1 Introduction and summary
2 Europe, which Europe?
3 The transformatin of Western Europe
4 The dynamics of integration
5 Direction and indirection: the processes of change
6 Forty years on

## The author

William Wallace is a Senior Research Fellow at St Antony's College, Oxford. He was previously Deputy Director of the Royal Institute of International Affairs.

## RIIA/PINTER PUBLISHERS